LOVE, TROUBLE & AMERICANO

VINCENT J HALL II

PRAISE FOR LOVE, TROUBLE & AMERICANO

"An all-too-real saucy tale of what happens when you don't avert your eyes at something shiny. Vincent J. Hall II is fantastic at telling a story. His characters are all people you probably know, and the enemy is an invisible force I believe all of us have been plagued with at least once in our lives. It's a must-read, for sure."

— John Queor, Author of *Bypass*

"*Love, Trouble & Americano* captures that very human urge to look past the life we already have to the life that could have been. It aptly examines the lies we tell—to others, and to ourselves—just to feel alive, and the fallout that results. Through Albert's story, Vincent J. Hall II skillfully forces the reader to recognize the times they've taken their own life for granted—a revelation that's bound to be equal parts unsettling and illuminating."

— Cortney Casey, Author of *Harrison's for the Holidays*

"An honest insight into how different people perceive relationship boundaries and an essential guide for those looking to distinguish love from lust. Vincent expertly combines the comfort of a long-term relationship with an adrenaline-inducing crush."

— Terry Lander, Author of *Monster Jackpot*

"*Love, Trouble & Americano* starts out as a relatable story about what happens when two people grow apart, but quickly turns into the tale about a mess of a man who just can't get his priorities straight. Written by the talented Vincent J. Hall II, this is an incredibly well-crafted, easy read with all sorts of little details and descriptions packed within. I personally enjoyed each and every turn in the story and getting to know the disaster that is Albert!"

— Matt Nickles, Author of *We Were Fire in the Night*

INDIE EARTH
PUBLISHING

LOVE, TROUBLE & AMERICANO

Vincent J. Hall II

Other Works By Vincent J. Hall II

The Drinks Between Us

Vincent J. Hall II has also been featured in

Glow: Self-Care Poetry for the Soul
A Winter's Warmth: Short Stories To Keep The Cold Away

"But it was just my imagination, once again
Runnin' away with me
Tell you, it was just my imagination
Runnin' away with me"

Just My Imagination (Running Away with Me)
The Temptations

LOVE, TROUBLE & AMERICANO

PART ONE

CHAPTER 1

Albert woke up agitated. He had already snoozed his alarm countless times and knew he was running late for work. Reluctantly, he threw on gray dress pants and a button-up shirt he had failed to notice had a stain, taming his short, dark hair with his fingers through his reflection in the bedroom TV. Looking in the bathroom mirror, his girlfriend Stacy worked calmly on her make-up, matching the coral blush of her cheeks to the natural red of her hair. The color made her hazel eyes pop as she stood just over five feet in a sunflower-printed sundress.

"Morning, baby," Stacy said, poking her head out through the doorway. "You better hurry or you're going to miss your train."

"Good morning, sweetie. I know. I'm leaving now."

"Don't forget we're meeting Rachel and Hunter for dinner this weekend."

"What? I don't remember agreeing to that. I don't want to go," he responded, rolling his brown eyes, trying to put on a tie and deciding not to wear one.

"Whatever, Albert. I told you about this," she said, a twang of irritation in her voice. "I think you're being childish," she popped back.

"Whatever, fine. I have to go," he said.

Albert grabbed his backpack and started walking toward

---

the door.

"I will see you tonight. Bye, love you," he said without looking back.

"Love you too," Stacy said as Albert walked out.

He closed the door to his suburban townhome, an adorable house with black shutters, a bay window, and a white door.

I really don't remember agreeing to that, he thought as he walked the few blocks to the train station, angry for letting himself get roped into another dinner with Stacy's college friends.

He always felt awkward around them and felt Rachel didn't like him very much. He knew Stacy would be annoyed all day about his refusal to attend the dinner and that it would probably start another fight between them. He never knew how to bite his tongue, a trait he got from his father—so quick to make a remark before weighing the consequences. Deciding to deal with it later, Albert was determined to get through the day without any more distractions.

An account executive at an investment firm, Albert was an average worker. He only worked as hard as he needed to, but he was charming, trustworthy, and had a way of getting people to agree with him that made him good at his job. Most days, he avoided doing actual work by sitting in his office, watching videos on his phone, which was leaned against his laptop screen, hoping someone wouldn't interrupt him with something important. This was normally when his boredom would force him to walk about the building—his nervous energy only allowing him to sit still for so long. His office was in a towering skyscraper in the city, and he would often stop on other floors and roam around, looking into open offices now and then. After a few laps around the building, Albert would end his trip at the ground-floor café. Every day, he would treat himself to an Americano.

———————————

That was when he first noticed her. She was at the café with her headphones on, typing away on her laptop. Something about her mesmerized him, and he began stuttering as he ordered his drink, sneaking glances back at her while the barista made his coffee. She was dressed in high-waisted wide-leg jeans, a white form-fitted shirt, and a black blazer that complimented her slender body. Her long blonde hair fell down her back, and as she got up to leave, he couldn't help following her around the lobby with his eyes. Albert grew so distracted, he hadn't heard what the cashier said.

"Sir, your coffee," the cashier repeated.

"I'm sorry... Yes, thank you," he said as he shook his head.

Still, in a daze, Albert walked toward the elevators, burning his tongue on his coffee as he thought about how gracefully she had moved across the room, like a ballroom dancer.

Who is she? he thought.

He stood there, distractedly riding the elevator. The doors opened and almost closed before Albert noticed he'd reached his floor. He stuck his hand out, catching the door, and moved toward his office like a zombie. He couldn't help the train of questions and thoughts racing through his head just as his heart was racing in his chest.

What does she do? Is she someone important, like a writer or a lawyer? How could I ever get close to her? Is she out of my league? She seems out of my league. If only I could have a moment with her, but I'm sure I would ruin it with my mumbling the whole time.

Albert pulled his chair out from his desk, devoid of any personal effects. The only things on top were his work laptop, a placemat, a mouse pad, and a pencil holder. He sat down and began running his fingers through his hair, still thinking about the woman downstairs. He busied himself with work to get her out of his mind.

A few minutes into responding to emails, his phone vibrated, it was a text from Stacy—**Sorry for this morning, I wasn't in a great mood. I hope your day gets better**—reminding him about the argument he had with her before he left the house.

He wondered if she was right and if he was genuinely childish or if she was exaggerating. He tried to continue with his work, constantly checking the clock to see when it was five. He would then be free to run out the door, free to think about the woman in the café.

At five, Albert made his way back downstairs; the café was closed and the building was nearly empty. It was spring and daylight was still shining in Center City, Philadelphia. Instead of taking his normal train, Albert decided to take a walk in Rittenhouse Square Park before heading to the station, thinking the walk would help clear his mind before the trip home. He loved the way the park looked this time of year. The trees swaying in the wind, music playing, people hanging out in the middle of the park by the fountain, sitting on the benches reading books, or watching the children run around and climb on the big lion sculpture. Leaves fell on his back as he thought about his relationship with Stacy. It had been almost seven years since they first met and so much time had passed since that day.

The two had met on an internet dating app, chatting for a few months before meeting in person. The first time they met was in a Starbucks a few blocks from Albert's office. He was nervous, but Stacy's energy made him feel comfortable. On their first formal date, Albert took Stacy to the Chinese Lantern Festival in Franklin Square and then for drinks at a beer garden.

He dismissed those thoughts as he made his way through

the park, gazing around as couples sat cuddled on benches, lovers locked in an eternal embrace, eyes trained on each other like a hunter to his prey.

Albert had a few more blocks to walk, and thirty minutes later, he arrived at his house. He slowed his pace as he reached his street, wanting to savor the moment. His last thought as he walked up the steps was the woman in the café.

As he reached for the doorknob, he tried to put the argument with Stacy behind him. He didn't want to start the evening on a bad note. He walked in to the sound of music and scented candles. He knew Stacy had been home for an hour and could see she'd decided to treat herself to some *me-time.*

"I opened a bottle of wine; I thought we could have the rest with dinner tonight," she said as she walked toward Albert.

"Works for me. What are you in the mood for?" he asked, dropping his backpack by the bedroom door.

"I don't know. You pick this time," she said as she kissed him on the cheek and started dancing around the room.

"Fine, pizza. Can you order? I want to hop in the shower."

Stacy ignored Albert and continued dancing as he got undressed and walked into the bathroom.

"Did you hear me?" he asked.

"Yeah, in a minute. You're not going to die, are you?"

"Possibly…" he said as he closed the door and turned on the shower.

"You'll be fine," she said as she continued dancing for a few more minutes before ordering the food.

Albert finished his shower and put on a pair of sweatpants and a T-shirt to sit on the couch. He looked at Stacy as she sat watching videos on her phone, her feet perched on the oak

<hr>

LOVE, TROUBLE & AMERICANO

coffee table. She was watching something funny because her laughter filled the room. He couldn't help but smile wider

"What are you looking at?" she said as she looked up from her phone.

"You… You're beautiful," he said honestly.

"Yeah, whatever. Don't think I forgot about what you said before you left," she said, getting up from the couch to answer the door.

"Fuck…" Albert whispered to himself.

"Huh?" she said, handing a twenty to the delivery guy and closing the door.

"Nothing… I'll grab plates and the bottle of wine," he said.

"That's what I thought," she said to herself jokingly as she walked back to the couch.

They sat in silence for a few moments, Albert thinking about what to say next, not wanting to start a fight. He opened the bottle of red wine and poured himself a glass. He refilled her glass and placed the bottle back on the table. She looked at him with a face that said, "Don't start with me," as she put a slice of sausage and peppers pizza on her plate.

"What should we watch?" she asked.

"Your choice," he said.

"Good answer," she said as she picked up the remote and started searching for a movie to watch.

CHAPTER 2

The next morning Albert woke up and realized Stacy was still asleep next to him. He laid in bed for a moment before getting up, not wanting a repeat of the previous day. Trying not to wake Stacy, Albert got out of bed slowly.

Stacy managed a jewelry and accessory consignment shop named Azul that was growing and she was in charge of every aspect, which meant she was always at the shop. This was the first time she'd gotten to sleep in a very long time.

He grabbed his clothes out of the closet, got dressed, and started packing his backpack by the door. Before Albert could put it on his back, Stacy rolled over to greet him.

"You're up early," she said, rubbing her eyes.

"Yeah, there's a report I forgot to file, and I want to get in early to send it," he said, reaching for the bedroom door. "I may be a little late tonight."

"Who is this new guy in front of me? Getting up early and working hard on reports," she said, sarcastically, her voice heavy with sleep.

"What?" he replied.

"Nothing... It looks good on you," she said, laying her head back down on the pillow.

Albert closed the bedroom door, stepped out of the house,

walked the few blocks to the train station, and waited patiently on the platform. He stood there staring at the gray and white tiles that lead up to the yellow strip before the track, bright letters printed on the floor that read 'Stand Back.' He surveyed the room, most people wearing work clothes. A man in a dress coat and very fancy loafers was seated to the left of him tapping his foot to the music in his headphones. On the adjoining side of the bench, a woman was reading a book, using her bookmark to follow along. Feeling like he'd been staring for too long, he moved his gaze to the other side of the platform looking at the electric sign that read '10 minutes till the next Eastbound train.'

The train arrived and Albert grabbed the first seat he could find. He had a good feeling he was going to see the woman in the café again. He smiled the whole ride into the office thinking about her, trying not to think about the lie he had told Stacy about the report. He couldn't lay in bed anymore and wanted to get to the office as soon as possible.

I wondered if she would be there during my break... I bet she has a fancy apartment in the city and an interesting job that lets her do whatever she wants.

The train reached his stop and Albert stepped out with the rest of the masses. Up on the street, it was a chilly autumn day and Albert was so excited to reach the office that he forgot a jacket. He shivered as he walked down the block to Four Penn Center, the large building covered entirely with glass windows. He enjoyed the fall and loved his walks when it was just warm enough but hated how the temperature fluctuated so much. He distracted himself from the weather by thinking about the mysterious, beautiful woman and the actual work he had to do. Even though he had lied about the report, Albert did have a large project he was in the middle of and it wasn't an inconvenience that he was at the office early.

He opened the door to the building and walked through a narrow hallway to the lobby, showing his ID to Walter, the portly security guard with coke-bottle glasses and a mustache who didn't move as he watched TV at the obnoxiously large granite front desk. He made his way to the elevator where a woman was already waiting. Albert looked over and noticed it was the woman from the café.

"Good morning," she said as she looked over at Albert who was standing there awkwardly.

"Hey… yeah, good morning," he said as the bell rang and the elevator door opened.

He stepped in and hit the button for the fourth floor. He looked up as she reached over him to push the button for the sixth floor and stepped back. They stood there quietly, Albert's heart pounding as he stared at the numbers as they lit up. He was avoiding eye contact with the mysterious woman, who was standing there not paying attention to him, but with her eyes on her phone. The bell rang again and the door opened on Albert's floor. He stood there for a second longer before walking off the elevator and down the hall to his office.

Wow, she's so beautiful... I can still smell her hair, fresh lavender, and spring, he thought.

He walked down the hall still in a daze. He opened the door to the front office.

I should go down later and see if she's there, he thought, already asking himself what kind of coffee she liked to drink. *Maybe she likes tea...*

He walked past the receptionist, a young woman wearing a dark gray knitted sweater and black jeans, her hair in a tight bun on the top of her head, and stopped for a moment.

"Morning, Steph, how are you?" Albert asked.

"Good, my boyfriend and I went axe throwing last night."

"Wow, that's exciting. I doubt I could trust myself throwing an axe," he replied with a laugh.

"I thought the same thing, but it's fun! Cathartic in a way. You should try it sometime. I'll email you the name of the place," she replied, already pulling up a link to the website to send Albert.

"Thanks, Steph."

He continued his way to his office, closed the door behind himself, and sat down at his desk, the whole time not even thinking about his motions. He sat back in his chair, putting his hands on his head, interlocking his fingers, and closed his eyes, trying to picture her face again. He imagined the way her hair settled around her shoulders as she stood next to him in the elevator. They were a few feet apart, but he could feel her body heat. A few minutes later, still lost in thought, Albert sat up abruptly, hearing the alert go off on his phone. It was a calendar notification reminding him there was a meeting he was supposed to lead in the conference room. He stood there for a second, shook his head, snapped out of his daze, and ran to the conference room to start his presentation.

"Good morning, everyone. Let's get started..." he said, opening the door.

After about an hour, he finished his presentation, and as people left, Albert stood there for a few more moments staring out the window at the horizon, the blue sky full of opportunities. It was a little too early for his normal walk and as he opened the door to his office again, he was once more confronted with thoughts of the mysterious woman. She'd left his mind for a moment, but now she was back.

He forced himself to push the thoughts aside, his phone vibrating in his pocket. It was a text from Stacy.

Hey, I may stay at the store a little longer today since I came in late. Let me know when you head home. Btw, Rach picked El Vez for dinner tomorrow night. I love you.

Albert read the message and put the phone back in his pocket, once again dreading the dinner he didn't recall ever agreeing to. He sent a few follow-up emails and the presentation notes. Checking off the two tasks, Albert sat back in his chair and wondered if he should start working on the report he had to do or if he should forego that to daydreaming about the mysterious woman.

With a sigh, he opened a Word document and began setting up the template for the report. Concentrated on margins, logistics, and the mundane details he needed to write about, Albert had not even realized it was time for his break until his alarm went off. He finished the report and sent it, pushing back his chair with such excitement that it slammed against the wall. He walked across the room to the door with a renewed spirit. He continued down the hall, passed the front office and out the door toward the elevator, the whole time with a spring in his step. His finger pushed the up button as if he was punching an opponent in the ring.

Come on... Come on... Let's go! he thought as he paced waiting for the door to open. *I wonder what she does here?*

Albert walked into the elevator, pushed the button for the sixth floor, and took a few steps back, leaning against the wall. He looked up and stared at the reflection of himself in the mirrored ceiling. He wished he'd worn a better suit today. He hadn't expected to run into the mysterious woman from the café and was trying to iron out the wrinkles on his shirt with his hands. The door opened to people waiting to get on as Albert made a mental note to dress better the next day. He walked past them, down the hall, stopping for a moment to look at the placard of each business on the floor. There were a few insurance and real estate companies

---

LOVE, TROUBLE & AMERICANO

and some unlabeled offices. He peaked through the windows, noticing displays for a magazine in one office and a law firm in another.

She has to work for one of these companies. Maybe she's a lawyer. I bet she is working hard on a brief or closing argument for a murder case, just like Jack McCoy in an episode of Law & Order, he thought.

Having looked around, Albert made his way to the end of the hall, stopping for a moment to look out at the sun shining through the window. As he closed his eyes, he could feel the sun warm his eyelids. He stood there with his hands clasped and his head back, relishing in the moment before making his way back to the elevator. Albert was not about to get his hopes up, but the way things were turning out for him, even if he bet on the worst horse, it could come up winning.

What am I wasting time for? She's probably already downstairs, he thought, frantically pushing the down button for the elevator. *I hope she doesn't leave before I get there. I don't know when the next time I'll see her is.*

He stood there staring as each number illuminated before hearing the sound of the elevator arriving. As the door opened, Albert stepped back in, pushed the lobby button, and slid his body against the wall as he waited to travel the few floors downstairs hoping his love affair would be there. He was looking at the numbers change when he remembered the text from Stacy. He opened his phone and started texting her back.

Okay, babe. No problem.

He stared at the text before sending it. This was the first time he'd thought about Stacy all day.

He pushed send—adding an **I love you** to ignore the guilt growing in his stomach—and put his phone back in his pocket.

———

The door opened to the lobby and he stepped off swiftly. He walked past the lobby desk to the entrance of the café, where he could hear the noise of the espresso machine grinding up the coffee beans, the aroma hitting his face. As he stepped in, he noticed the mysterious woman was in line to order a drink. He jumped in line behind her, silently excited, and pretended to look up at the menu board. As they stood there waiting for the barista to finish making the order, she turned around, looked at the line behind her, and made eye contact with Albert. He smiled and she turned to face him.

"You were in the elevator with me this morning, right?" she asked.

"Yeah, I have a very *exciting* job on the fourth floor."

"Oh, cool," she said, turning back around to the register to order her coffee.

"I'll have a medium, iced Americano, please, and thank you," she said, reaching into her wallet for her debit card.

Albert chuckled to himself, surprised that someone else disliked the bitterness of coffee like him.

"You like Americanos too?" he asked.

"Yeah, they're great when you need a pick-me-up."

He ordered his drink and they both stepped aside to wait for their orders to come.

"I'm Albert, by the way," he said, extending his hand.

"Becca! Nice to meet you," she responded, shaking his hand.

Albert noticed how soft it was and thought about the last time he held hands with Stacy. It seemed like it had been forever ago.

A few moments later, the barista walked over with both of their drinks and placed them on the counter. They grabbed their coffees and made their way over to the tables. The café was bust-

———————————

bustling and most of the tables were full of people on their lunch break. Albert normally took his coffee to go, but he didn't want to miss an opportunity to talk more with Becca.

"Looks kind of busy… Would you mind sharing a table?" he asked.

"Sure," she said.

Albert sat down, trying to hold back his nerves. His heart was racing like it was going to jump out of his mouth.

Okay, stay cool, he thought.

Becca pulled out a book from her bag and placed it on the table before sitting down. He looked at the bright red book with large letters printed on the cover, *Rebecca*, then back at her.

"You're reading *Rebecca* and your name is Becca?" he said, sarcastically.

"Yes, I know it seems self-obsessed, but I've always been interested in it. The story is quite thrilling."

"What's it about?"

"Well, it's about a woman—you don't know her name—who ends up marrying a wealthy man who's just lost his wife, Rebecca. Then, she starts to notice that she's not alone in the quiet mansion… Things start to happen that she can't explain, and there's a constant eerie feeling there's a presence she can't see. It's really good if you're into gothic romances," she said, taking a sip of her coffee.

"I can't say that I am, but now you have me interested. I'll be sure to grab it the next time I'm in a bookstore," he said, his eyes pressed on her, fully engaged in the conversation.

"Sounds like you've read it before?" he added.

"Yeah, this is my second time reading it... It's always better the second time around. You find so many more details you missed the first time," she said, messing with the napkin undern-

———————

VINCENT J. HALL II

16

eath her coffee cup. "You don't seem like an avid reader."

"No, definitely not. I haven't picked up a book, willingly, since high school."

"You make it sound like torture."

"Just haven't found anything I'm interested in, until now… Besides I'm more of a movie guy. May I?" Albert said, picking up her book and flipping through the pages.

"It's worth reading if you want to give it a try."

He put the book back on the table and she picked it up, securing her bookmark before placing it back in her bag.

"What type of movies are you into?"

"It depends on the day, but mostly independent films or ones no one's ever heard of."

"Like what?"

"One of my favorites is *Doctor Zhivago*. It's not a gothic romance, but, in my opinion, one of the best love stories ever," he said, confidently as he picked up his cup to take a sip.

"I'll have to take your word for it," she replied.

Becca finished her coffee and picked up her phone from the table to check the time.

"I hate to cut this short, but I have to head back to work."

"No worries, I enjoyed this conversation," he said, smiling as he got up from his chair.

"Me too. It was nice talking with you," she said as she grabbed her bag, got up, and pushed in her chair.

Becca picked up her cup, which prompted Albert to do the same. They walked over to the counter, placed them down, and walked out the entrance of the café.

"Listen, the next time I'm down here, if you don't mind, I'll stop by and we can continue our conversation. I'm interested to hear what other books you're interested in," Albert said, hoping

Becca couldn't hear how loud his heart was beating as his pulse began to quicken.

"Sure, I'm always happy to chat about books," Becca said, smiling.

"Have a good weekend."

"You too."

Albert's clammy hand pushed the button for the elevator and they stood in the same spots they had earlier that morning.

I can't believe that happened, he thought to himself as the door of the elevator opened.

Reaching the floor to his office, he stepped off the elevator and walked back to his desk smiling to himself, almost giddy. He sat down in his chair, ruminating over every word of his conversation with Becca. He turned on his computer, his screen open to his calendar. He added Stacy's dinner plans made earlier in the week with her old college friends to his personal calendar, which made him more frustrated since he would be stuck dealing with them and would have to wait until Monday to see Becca. He sighed deeply, pushed in his chair, and decided to leave work early.

Taking the train home and having dinner by himself since Stacy had worked late was a blur. He was laying in bed staring at the ceiling, replaying his conversation with Becca in the café, wondering if she thought of him too.

What a gorgeous smile she had... It was like every word she said was perfect coming from her lips, and the way she looked at me—

"How was your day?" Stacy asked as she snuggled up next to him.

He had been so deep in thought that he had not even realized she had gotten out of the shower and had climbed into bed.

"Alright, the presentation went well. I think the clients

---

liked it," he said, adding to his lie.

"Nice job baby. I'm proud of you," she said, laying her head on his chest and her hand on his stomach.

"Thank you, sweetie," he said.

"Do you know what's coming up soon?" he added, looking up at the ceiling.

"No, what?" she answered, sleepily.

"Our anniversary."

"How do you always remember?"

"I put a reminder in my calendar for a month before," he admitted.

"And here I was thinking you remembered on your own," she said with a yawn.

He kissed her forehead, leaning over to turn off the black lamp with a white fracture line on it that stood on the nightstand.

———————————

CHAPTER 3

Albert woke up feeling disappointed. He knew he'd have to sit through a tedious dinner and was not excited about the whole idea. He wasn't a big fan of Stacy's friends. They had always made him feel like an outsider, but he didn't make an effort to join in either. Albert also thought about how he wouldn't see Becca again until Monday, and he couldn't wait, daydreaming about the chance to run into her in the city during the weekend.

He pushed his feelings aside, not wanting to become agitated before the day started. It was going to be a long day and Stacy fed off his energy and knew immediately when he was in a bad mood. They were both busy with work during the week, only leaving them a little time on the weekend to spend together.

Stacy had been up for a while and was enjoying her coffee on the couch in the living room. She loved the moments in the morning when it was quiet. She would open up the curtains to let the morning light in, light a candle, and place it on the dark black entertainment center. She could sit in the living room, flipping through the many coffee table books laid out, or walk over to the two bookshelves that lined the right side of the room and choose from dozens of novels she'd already read. Albert slowly sat up in the bed, rubbed his eyes, and then stood up to stretch. After a few seconds, he walked out of the bedroom into the living room where he saw Stacy sitting cross-legged on the couch with a book in her lap. He smiled to himself and then shook his head, pushing the thought of Becca and her book out of his mind.

"Good morning!" she said, cheerfully.

"Hey, babe... What time is it?" he asked.

"9:15."

"You didn't wake me," he said as he sat down on the couch next to her.

"No, I wanted you to sleep in so you wouldn't be so cranky later," she said sarcastically.

"You know me so well," he said, chuckling a little. "What are we doing today?"

"I have the whole day planned," she said excitedly as she placed the book back on the table.

"We're taking the train into the city to the art museum and maybe, if we have time, we can stop by a few antique shops on the way back," she said, getting up and walking toward the kitchen.

"Don't worry about making breakfast, we'll grab something on the way," she added as she put her cup in the sink.

"Alright, I'll get ready then," he said as he got up off the couch, standing tall and stretching his arms in the air.

As Albert started walking back to the bedroom, he crossed Stacy's path. He stopped and kissed her.

"I love you," he said, his face brightening as he looked at her.

"I love you too," she said, her eyes widening.

Albert smiled. He took a shirt and a pair of jeans out of his drawer and proceeded to get dressed. He walked back out to the living room to find his shoes as Stacy finished putting her things together. She grabbed her bag and began walking toward the door.

"Ready?" he said, bending down to grab his shoes from

under the table.

"Yeah, waiting on you."

Albert sat down to put on his shoes and grabbed his wallet and keys off the table before walking out the door. There was a light breeze in the air as they walked the few blocks to the train station. They swiped their train passes and walked up the steps to the platform. As they stood waiting, Albert put his head back, looked up at the sky, and closed his eyes to bask in the sunlight. Stacy looked at him and hoped his good mood would last the whole day. A few minutes later, the train arrived, they got on and found seats in the front of the car. It was a short ride into the city, and Albert sat staring out the window as the train slowly gained speed, the houses whooshing past them. He tried to clear his mind and concentrate on having fun with Stacy. He didn't want the distraction of Becca to ruin the day for them.

The train stopped abruptly and Albert and Stacy got up from their seats to disembark, Stacy grabbing Albert's hand as they walked across the platform toward the door. Out on the street, the city was bursting with excitement, people walking around, the sound of car horns honking in traffic, and the crisp air on their faces. Stacy threw up her hand to hail a cab while Albert stood next to her checking his emails on his phone.

"I ordered tickets online for the museum, so it should be pretty quick to get in," she said, waving her hand a little bit.

"Uh-huh," said Albert, not looking up from his phone.

Moments later, a taxi pulled up to the corner, Stacy stepped off the curb to open the door and had to stop to snap her fingers at Albert who was still wrapped up in his phone.

"Sorry babe, just wanted to check a few things," he said as he slid into the taxi and shut the door.

They arrived at the museum and walked up the huge steps

to the entrance. The building was massive, with large granite steps in the middle of the lobby that lead up to the other floors. It was built with high ceilings and contained large rooms with abstract expressionism and modern art from famous artists. Patrons flowed in and out of the cold, dimly lit spaces and a low murmur could be heard of people commenting on the symbolism of each painting. Stacy stood there, enveloped in a painting by Mark Rothko. She thought about the deep colors, the violet top, the black line in the middle, and how the yellow, and orange merged into each other. She loved how they pulled her into the painting.

Stacy hadn't moved since she first saw the painting. She was mesmerized, and almost felt like she couldn't stop staring at it. Albert—who wasn't a big fan of art, but knew Stacy was—putzed around the room quietly and quickly looking at each painting before moving on to the next one.

I kind of like what they did here, but I wouldn't put it in my house, he thought.

When he noticed that Stacy hadn't moved from her spot for a few minutes, he came up behind her, wrapped his arms around her, and kissed her on the cheek. Stacy only took her eyes off the painting after feeling the soft kiss.

"I really like this painting!" she said as Albert pulled her toward the other room.

"Yeah, I could tell."

"We should see if they have a print in the gift shop. It'd be nice to put up in our living room," she said, squeezing his hand as they walked through the gallery space.

"Sure thing, babe."

They walked a little more through the galleries, Stacy stopping at each painting, drinking in all the colors they had to offer. Albert, now ready to leave, was excited when they started

---

making their way to the lobby again. Remembering Stacy's love for the Rothko painting, he diverted their exit to search the gift shop for the print. Luckily, they had a few left in stock and he bought one for Stacy who was beaming as he handed it to her. She touched his arm softly.

"Thank you so much, baby," she said, still smiling as they walked out of the store.

"You're welcome, just don't let me catch you staring at it in the middle of the night!" he said, chuckling to himself.

"Funny!" she said, smacking him on the shoulder playfully.

"I just think it's really beautiful. What's wrong with that?"

"Nothing wrong with that at all, babe."

"Should we stop somewhere to grab something to eat?" Stacy asked as they walked back down the enormous steps that lead to the street.

"Yeah, please. Staring at those paintings made me hungry," he said sarcastically.

"I bet they did," she said, shaking her head.

At the bottom, Albert stopped for a second to search for the closest restaurant on his phone. The nearest one was less than a mile away and as they walked down the street, Stacy looked into different windows to see which places she might want to visit after they ate. Albert, seeing how joyful she was, didn't want to ruin the moment. He walked slowly next to her, giving her time to peek into each window.

"There are a few stores around here that have cute little kitschy stuff for sale."

"Yeah, you should be able to find something nice to go with your new painting," he smiled at her.

"Hopefully," she said, not acknowledging Albert's sarcasm.

They arrived at a quaint coffee shop with a huge wooden door and frosted glass in the middle. When they walked in, there was a white cold case that offered sandwiches and other assortments of juices and water. Opposite the cold case, he could see a glass case filled with different delicious French pastries. They stood in front of the white and gray marble counter that held the large chrome espresso machine for a few seconds looking at the menu board before getting in line to order. They ordered and, after paying, found one of the empty booths that lined the far wall and sat under one of the cliché pictures of Paris on the wall.

"What time are we supposed to meet Hunter and Rachel at the restaurant?" he asked.

"The reservation is for seven o'clock, I thought we could stop in a few shops before heading back home."

"Sounds good to me."

"Order ready for number 10," said the cashier, his voice ringing over the loudspeaker.

Albert jumped up to grab his turkey and Swiss panini and Stacy's cobb salad, famished at this point, and raced back to their table. They ate quietly, Albert thinking about the impending awkwardness that would come with their dinner plans. Stacy, just grateful to be spending time together with Albert. They finished eating and left the shop back on their adventure. They only walked a few feet before popping into the first store—a consignment shop that offered used items from the 80s and 90s.

It was bright in the shop, the fluorescent light almost blinding as they played electronica music. Albert, uninterested, walked to the back of the store to check out the men's section. Not finding anything, he returned to Stacy who was looking at the wall of cassette tapes. She stood there looking at the different band names and mixtapes people had made and donated to the store. Not finding a band she liked, Stacy turned and motioned to Albert that they could leave.

They popped in and out of two more shops, each one owned by a quirky shopkeeper who filled table after table with different dusty treasures that could be housed on a shelf or mantle. While walking in one of the stores, Stacy came upon a necklace with a moon pendant. She picked it up, stared at it for a few moments, then put it down. Albert wondered if the pendant was something that Stacy wanted, but the once-optimistic Stacy walked back to the station empty-handed.

"I saw you pick up that necklace, you didn't like it?" Albert asked.

"I did, but it was a little too expensive," she replied, slightly disappointed.

"Maybe next time," he said, wanting to comfort her.

They walked back into the station, swiped their passes, and walked up the steps to the platform. On the way home, they sat quietly in their seats, both looking out the window, lost in their thoughts. Once back at home, they had an hour to get ready before leaving for dinner. Albert, who wasn't trying to impress her friends, sat on the couch watching videos on his phone while Stacy rushed around the house getting ready. He'd already planned what he was going to wear and only needed a couple of minutes to get dressed before they walked out the door.

"Since you're sitting there, call the cab and ask them to be here in 15 minutes," Stacy said, running back and forth from the bedroom to the bathroom.

"Okay, babe," he said loudly, making sure she heard him from the other room.

Albert made the call and then went back to watching vid-

———————————

eos on his phone.

"Are you going to get dressed?" she asked, getting annoyed he was just sitting there.

"Yeah, in a minute... You know it doesn't take me that long to get dressed," he said, plugging the charger in his phone and getting off the couch.

He walked back to the bedroom and opened the closet to take out one of the options he'd picked to wear for Becca. He dressed quickly, leaving the tie on the bed, but keeping the jacket on. Then, he walked back to the living room to wait. Stacy was standing in the middle of the living room, wearing a white and yellow polka dot sundress and sandals, trying to rearrange the items in her bag while holding it in midair. Albert looked up, noticing how beautiful she looked. Outside, the taxi pulled up to the front of the house and honked its horn twice.

They walked out the door, Stacy still holding her bag in her hand. Albert opened the car door, letting Stacy in, then shut the door behind her and walked to the other side. She gave the driver the address to the trendy Mexican restaurant El Vez, which was roughly 20 minutes away from their house. They would be there just in time to make the reservation, not to mention the taxi driver was driving a little erratically, speeding through every yellow light.

Once there, Stacy texted her friends to see if they'd been seated yet, which they had. They made their way through the noisy restaurant, people chatting and the waitstaff zipping around tables carrying large trays of food on their palms. They made their way to the table in the corner where her friends were sitting, who were talking low to each other when they walked up.

"Hey!" they said, almost in unison.

"Hi, guys," Stacy said as she took out her chair to sit.

———————————

Rachel looked across the table at Albert as he sat down.

"What's going on, Albert?" she asked.

"Not much. How've things with you two?" he asked, trying to start the conversation light.

"Busy as usual. My practice has been picking up," Rachel said, looking at Hunter.

Rachel was a therapist and would sometimes mention to Albert that she would make a referral for him if he ever wanted to talk to someone. Albert felt she'd never liked him since the first day they met and she would occasionally shoot a dirty look at Albert, which he tried to ignore.

"How about you, Hunter?" he asked.

"Nothing too crazy, opening up another bakery next month."

"That's awesome, man. Congratulations," Albert replied, forcing a smile.

"Yeah, that makes three now, right?" Stacy asked.

"Yup, it's a lot of work, but I love it," he replied, picking up the menu.

Albert did the same, wanting to avoid conversation for a moment. The waiter came to take their order, and after ordering, they sat waiting for their food to come before Rachel broke the silence.

"So what did you two do today?" Rachel asked, putting her phone down.

"We had a nice day," Stacy said, putting her hand on Albert's, who had put his phone down and re-entered the dinner party mentally.

"Yeah, we walked around the museum for a couple of hours, looking at beautiful art, then stopped at a coffee shop for a bite to eat before going shopping," he said with enthusiasm.

"Sounds like a lovely day, '' Rachel said, sarcastically.

"Did you hear Sara is getting married?" she added, looking at Stacy, switching the conversation.

There was an intensity to her tone, an intention to the sudden change of topic.

"They've only been together for less than a year," Stacy said softly, looking directly at Albert, who only knew of Sara in passing.

"Wow, that's pretty quick, don't you think?" Albert said, looking back at Stacy.

"I don't think so, not when two people are in love," Rachel said, interrupting Stacy who was about to answer.

"I mean, it still feels a bit early to me. Rachel and I got married after dating for three years, but I do love her more every day," Hunter said, kissing Rachel's cheek.

Albert forced a half-hearted smile and looked over at Stacy, sliding his hand over hers beneath the table.

"Sara's thinking about using the same shop I used, Demure Bridal to buy her wedding dress and she already asked me to be a bridesmaid. I'm sure she'll ask you next," Rachel said.

Albert looked around the room, trying to avoid eye contact. When his eyes met back with Rachel's again, she looked at him with what Albert interpreted as a more devious look.

The server arrived with a large tray of tacos, nachos with pico de gallo, and enchiladas placed it down on the opposite table, and began to put out each person's plate.

"Oh my god, this food looks amazing," Stacy said.

Albert agreed, nodding his head as he unwrapped his utensils.

The table was quiet for a few minutes as everyone started their meal, forks, and knives clinking on their plates until Rachel broke the silence.

She sat forward placing her hand on her chin, "When are you two getting married?" she asked, smiling, looking directly at Albert.

He took a bite of his quesadilla and choked on the gooey cheese, taking a sip of water before answering. He assumed that Rachel asked about marriage on purpose, tried to lighten the mood, and acted like he needed to think about it.

Upon his silence, Stacy turned to look at Albert with a face that said, "Hurry up and you better have the right answer!"

"I don't know, what's the rush?" he said, trying to be funny.

Stacy took her hand off Albert's, shifting in her chair.

"Really?" she said.

"What! I was joking?" he said, gritting his teeth and making a face.

Stacy sat there for a second, unable to speak. She was so taken aback. For the first time, she was questioning their relationship. They had already been together for seven years, and it was not that she was expecting to get married that weekend, but she also thought he'd be more committed to the idea than that.

Hunter, reading the room, quickly changed the conversation to decrease the tension at the table.

"What's new with you, Albert?" Hunter asked.

"I just got into golf. My boss took me out the other day for a round," he said.

"Are you any good?"

"Not really, but I loved hitting balls at the driving range."

"Yeah, that's always the best, smacking them down the green," Hunter said, grinning.

"And my short game is getting better," Albert replied,

grateful for Hunter having his back.

"Nice, we should hit the links one day. There's a place I know nearby that's great!" Hunter said excitedly.

Noticing the two men bonding, Stacy excused herself to the bathroom and Rachel followed, giving her a chance to talk about Albert.

Hunter waited until Rachel was far enough from the table to say, "Listen, don't pay her any mind, Rachel's just being Rachel... It's not you... This is just how she is."

"I'll try not to," Albert nodded, looking at Hunter.

Albert sat back in his chair, feeling a little more relaxed after Hunter's comment. A few moments later, Stacy and Rachel walked back from the bathroom, their laughter replacing the silence at the table. As Stacy sat down, she shot Albert a subtle dirty look, which worried him. He didn't think she took his joke that seriously.

"How about dessert?" Hunter asked.

"I think we're going to end the night a little early... I have to get up early tomorrow," Stacy said.

"Okay, no worries, I'll get the check and we can head out."

Hunter got up to speak to the server, paid the bill, and walked back to the table.

"Awe, thank you, guys. Next time, we'll treat."

"Yeah, thank you, man," Albert added.

By this time, everyone was standing and Rachel came around the table to hug Stacy, while Hunter and Albert stood there. Hunter patted Albert on the back.

"Remember what I said... It's just the way she is," he said, softly before extending his hand to give him a handshake.

"Alright, this was great! Let's do it again soon, yeah?"

LOVE, TROUBLE & AMERICANO

Rachel said as they walked toward the door.

"Absolutely," Albert said, struggling to get the word out of his mouth.

Stacy looked at Rachel and mouthed "I'll call you later."

As they stood outside waiting for the cab, Albert stared at his phone, at nothing in particular, just trying to avoid eye contact with Stacy who was standing off to the side, still upset with him after his response. When the taxi arrived, Stacy pushed past Albert to get in first, sliding to the other side and facing the window. The entire ride she never looked at Albert who was trying to remember every word he'd said at dinner.

What's her problem? It's not like I said never! he thought.

When they arrived home, Stacy opened the door and walked directly to the living room table to drop her bag and then straight back to the bedroom, slamming the door behind her. Albert turned on the lights and sat on the couch, grabbing the remote to turn on the TV. This was the first time they'd been in a fight over marriage. Albert knew to give her space and eventually, she would realize that he hadn't said he wouldn't marry her. Twenty minutes later, Stacy walked back out in her pajamas and sat on the further side of the couch.

"Are you still ignoring me? Why are you so upset?" Albert asked.

"It's been seven years, Albert... You're never going to ask me," Stacy said, tiredness in her voice. "What are we doing here then if you don't plan to marry me?"

Albert, who had been leaning forward clicking through the channels while Stacy was talking, sat back on the couch, placing the remote next to him.

"Come on, you know I love you... Do we have to plan our whole future tonight?"

<hr>

"Not the whole future Albert, just the next step," said Stacy, who got up off the couch, walked to the hall closet, and started taking out pillows and blankets.

She placed them in a neat pile next to the door and walked down the hall. Albert heard the bedroom door lock as Stacy closed it behind her.

Albert walked over and grabbed the pillows and blankets, shocked about what happened in the last few minutes. He was sure tomorrow they'd be fine.

Who am I kidding? She's making me sleep out here, Albert thought.

He dropped the bedding on the couch and laid down, placing his head on the big pile and stretching his legs out, extending his feet off the side. Albert allowed himself to get into his head.

Why are we in a rush? So what, we've been together for seven years. Who makes the rules on when you're supposed to get married anyways? I thought it was when you were both ready... Whatever, she'll get over it...

CHAPTER 4

Albert awoke to the sound of Stacy slamming the cabinet door shut in the kitchen.

"What's with all the noise?" he asked, half asleep.

"Nothing, I'm making coffee," she responded quickly.

"Do you have to be so loud about it?" he asked.

"Albert, I'm not in the mood... It doesn't matter because I'm leaving in a few minutes."

Albert pulled the blankets off his body and sat up on the couch while Stacy stood at the counter, the coffee machine loudly producing steam in front of her. He walked into the kitchen and felt Stacy avoiding his gaze as she stood there staring at the liquid dripping into her travel mug. When it was finished, she closed the lid on top and walked past Albert trying to ignore the confused look he was giving her.

"What are your plans for the day?" he asked, still looking at her as she finished putting her things together and grabbing her bag.

"I'm going out."

He sighed and walked back to the couch.

"Okay. I guess I'll see you later," he mumbled mostly into the pillow.

"Yup," she said sternly, opening the door to leave.

Albert sighed deeply after hearing the door slam shut. He moved the blankets around to find the remote, turned on the TV, and sat back on the couch in his thoughts for a moment.

I can't believe she's still pissed. When is this going to end? Maybe if I plan a date night she'll forgive me…

He suddenly remembered the conversation with Steph about axe-throwing and leaned forward to grab the laptop on the coffee table. He opened it up and logged into his work email to look for the link. When the site came up, there was a button at the top to book a reservation. He looked at the calendar and saw that, conveniently, Wednesday still had a few slots available. He booked a spot, picked up his phone to create a reminder, and opened up a new tab to start looking up easy recipes to make for dinner. Albert wasn't a chef, but he knew he had to do a little more than just book a reservation to get Stacy to forgive him.

He continued searching until he found a creamy Tuscan chicken dish he thought they both might like and knew he couldn't mess up. Feeling like he had a plan, he got up from the couch, folded the blankets, then walked over to the closet to put the spare pillows back. Albert dressed to head to the grocery store, hoping to get back and get started before Stacy came home.

It was a little chilly out so when Albert walked out of the house, he immediately turned around to grab a jacket. The town he lived in had one main street and, on weekends, there was always a farmer's market. Albert had a few other things he wanted to do before buying the food for dinner. He thought it would be a good idea to find a stall with flowers. He didn't remember the kind Stacy liked but thought she'd appreciate the gesture regardless of what type of flowers he got. He bought a dozen yellow roses since the cashier at the stall said they were supposed to represent for-giveness.

LOVE, TROUBLE & AMERICANO

He strolled down the street, stopping every few stalls to look at the different tables filled with fresh fruit and vegetables—each one more tantalizing than the next. They looked delicious; the bright colors jumping off the table enticed him. Albert stopped in front of one vendor, pulling his phone out of his pocket and checking the recipe. It called for cherry tomatoes and baby spinach. Albert surveyed all the stalls around him. It took him a few moments before finding the one he needed—one he'd passed when he first walked down the block. It was a large white stall with a blue sign that said 'Fresh Veggies' and had cartoonish carrots painted next to the words. There were two young kids and a man working.

"Hi, how are you? Quick question," Albert began.

"Hey, what can I do for you?"

"I need cherry tomatoes and baby spinach, do you have them?"

"Yes, we have them in half and full pounds. How much do you need?" the man asked, grabbing a plastic bag to collect them.

"Just a half pound please."

"And what about baby spinach?"

"The same, half, please. How much do I owe you?" Albert asked, reaching into his back pocket for his wallet.

"Five dollars, sir," he answered as he handed Albert the bags.

Albert smiled as he took the bags, looking over at the kids who were busy working behind their father.

The father looked up at Albert.

"Part-time job... A good way for them to earn a little money," he answered.

"Right," Albert said, nodding his head.

He walked away thinking about the last time he had a summer job. He'd wanted a drum set and his parents couldn't aff-

---

ord it. So, he mowed lawns for an entire summer just to save up for it. In the end, he asked his parents to take him to the store to buy the bright blue kit with chrome trim. He spent the next few months hammering away at those drums with no end in sight. As he walked away, he laughed to himself remembering how annoyed his parents got at how loudly he would play.

Albert returned home ready to complete his mission. He placed all the ingredients out on the kitchen counter and opened his phone to start reading the recipe, which appeared ten times more difficult than it had when he first read it.

Why did I pick this? I can't make this. I should've just ordered something and made it look like I cooked, he thought, growing frustrated.

He took a deep breath and read it over again, trying to find his cool. Albert reached into the cabinet for the pan, placed it on the stove, then bent down at eye level with the burner to turn it on. After a few moments, he poured in the oil before adding in the chicken and seasonings. Wanting to get in the cooking mood and since the chicken had a few minutes to cook, Albert looked for some jazz music to play on his phone. He picked his favorite song to start with: "Take Five" by Dave Brubeck. He tapped his feet as he shook the pan to move the chicken around.

Next, he pulled out the butter from the refrigerator and cut an inch-sized piece, and tossed it into the skillet. He grinned as he heard the sizzle in the pan, then reached for the garlic and cherry tomatoes. He took a handful and placed them on the cutting board, chopping them in half before adding them to the skillet. The entire kitchen was filled with an utterly mouthwatering aroma, and it was at this moment he heard the door open and close between the cracking of the oil and the saxophone on his phone.

"Hey, I'm home... Smells good in here," Stacy said, almost surprised.

"Yeah, trying out a new recipe. I'll be done in a little bit," Albert yelled from the kitchen.

"Okay, I'm going to hop in the shower real quick."

Stacy walked into the kitchen to see Albert moving like a pro. He turned around to see her standing there staring. He shook the pan one more time, then walked over to the table to hand Stacy the flowers.

"Got you these."

"What's all this for?" she asked, already knowing, but wanting to hear Albert say it out loud.

"To say I'm sorry... I didn't say we'd never get married. I shouldn't have joked. I do care about you and I think we should talk about our future more," he said, coming closer to Stacy and putting his arms around her.

He kissed her, hoping his gesture would land with her and she would forget about the fight.

She smiled, then playfully slapped him on the shoulder.

"Don't burn the food, I'm hungry!" she said, walking out of the kitchen towards the bedroom.

Albert jumped back in front of the stove, added the last ingredients—heavy cream and parmesan—and turned the heat down to a simmer. He pulled out the plates from the cabinet and began setting the table.

As the music continued playing loudly in the background, he swayed back and forth. Bopping to the beat, he placed the plates down, then danced back over to grab the utensils from the drawer. He had a few more minutes before the food was done cooking and placed the flowers in a vase from under the sink, putting them in the center of the table, and adjusting them to make sure they were perfect.

The whole house smelled incredible as Stacy emerged from the bedroom, hair wet, in a tank top and leggings.

"I can't believe you did all this, babe," she said, pulling out a chair and sitting at the table.

"Now and then, I can still amaze you," he said with a wry smile. "Want something to drink?"

"Yes, please," she said, turning her head slightly to face him.

"Water, tea, wine?" he asked, opening the refrigerator.

"Water is fine for now," she replied.

He took the pitcher out, then walked over to the cabinet door to grab two glasses. He poured the water and brought them over, placing one in front of Stacy and the other by his plate.

"Are you ready to eat?"

"Yeah, I'm starving! I forgot to eat lunch," she said.

"How'd you manage that?" Albert asked, reaching for a large spoon to serve the chicken.

"Just busy running around, I guess," she said.

He walked over with the pan still hot and began to dress her plate with a creamy sauce and a large golden brown chicken breast, topped with cherry tomatoes.

"On second thought, I will have a glass of wine to go with this fantastic-looking dinner you made."

Albert chuckled.

"Thanks for the compliment, but you haven't eaten it yet," he said as he plated his dish.

"Yeah, I know, but it looks phenomenal."

"You know what? You're doing all the work. Let me grab

<hr>

the bottle, sit down and eat your food," Stacy said, rising from her chair.

"I got it, don't worry," he said, pulling out a bottle from the cabinet above the stove, then walking back over to the table.

Placing the glasses down, he uncorked the bottle and started to pour white wine into each of them. He looked at her, soaking in the moment before taking a seat, and placing the bottle next to the vase in the middle of the table. The jazz music still playing on his phone on the counter, Chet Baker singing "Almost Blue," set the mood for the evening. All that was missing were candles and it would have been a scene right out of a movie.

It was quiet for a few minutes, both of them intently eating their meal, communicating only through eye contact. Albert was sure his plan had worked, smiling as he put a piece of chicken in his mouth.

She couldn't still be mad after all this. Dinner, flowers, jazz. Come on!

Stacy lightly smiled with her eyes, looking at Albert's face full of satisfaction. She'd decided earlier that day that she wasn't mad at Albert but that she wasn't going to let him off the hook that easily either. This was a step in the right direction.

"How do you like it?"

"It's amazing. Just as good as it looks," she said, half-jokingly, half-shocked at how good it was.

"Thanks, sweetheart," he said.

They continued their dinner and Stacy told him about all the places she went to in town, visiting different shops to look for new inspiration. When they were finished, Albert cleared the table, rinsed the dishes off before putting them in the dishwasher, then wiped down the counters before turning the light off. Stacy got up from the table and walked into the living room to sit on the couch.

She grabbed a blanket that was still out and covered them both up, moving closer so she could cuddle up next to him. He picked up the remote from the table and handed it to her. Albert sat there bracing himself for a few hours of mind-numbing reality TV but knew it was Stacy's favorite binge-show to watch on the weekends.

Later that evening, Albert, yawning and stretching in his seat, got up to go to bed. Stacy followed along after folding up the blanket and putting it back in the hall closet. She walked into the room where Albert was already taking off his clothes to change into his pajamas. She walked over to him, putting her hands on his back and kissing his shoulder. He turned around to face her, kissing her softly on the lips, then gently pushing her down on the bed. He climbed on top of her and began kissing her more. Their kisses became more passionate as they started to undress frantically. Albert kissed Stacy's neck as they began making love.

After they finished, he looked her in the eyes before kissing her softly again.

"I love you," Stacy said.

"I love you too," Albert said, kissing her forehead.

They both lay there for a few moments before Stacy got up to use the bathroom and Albert got up to get dressed again. She came back into the room, and as she got back into bed, he kissed her good night one more time.

———

PART TWO

CHAPTER 5

When Albert woke up the next morning, he looked over at Stacy, who was still sleeping and lay there momentarily thinking about the night before. He showered, and while standing there, the lukewarm water rolling down his back, he found himself going over the day ahead and thinking about Becca, hoping he would see her again. In his towel, with droplets of water landing on the wooden floor, he went to his closet, indecisively pulling out clothes, unsure of what the best outfit would be.

Stacy woke up startled by Albert staring at all the clothes laid out on his side of the bed.

"What are you doing? What are you getting dressed up for?"

"A few clients are coming into the office today. I want to look nice," he lied, avoiding eye contact.

She slid out of bed, trying not to disturb the collection of dress shirts and pants Albert couldn't decide between, but ultimately putting together a light blue shirt and tie combination for him.

"Here, wear this. You always look nice in this shirt," she said. "Let me know how it goes."

He stood there for a moment looking at the outfit his girlfriend threw together for him. He shook off the guilt as he dressed, kissing Stacy's cheek as he headed out the door.

As he walked to the train station, he thought of what Becca would think of his wardrobe but then was distracted by his phone vibrating in his pocket. It was a text from Stacy.

Aren't you forgetting something?

Shit, he thought, realizing he'd forgotten his bag at the house.

He turned around and started walking back at a fast pace, trying to not sweat through his shirt.

He texted Stacy.

Yes, can you leave it by the door? I'm running back now.

Albert rushed home, thinking about how he let someone he just met occupy his mind so much. He reached the steps to his house, still in thought. He opened the door and Stacy was there holding his bag.

"You okay?" she said.

"Huh," he said, reaching out to grab the bag.

"You're so distracted today. Are you sure everything is okay?" she asked, looking at Albert, who was checking train times on his phone.

"Yeah, I'm good. Just thinking about it a lot. I'll be fine once I get some coffee."

"Okay, well, good luck with the clients. I love you."

"Thank you, love you too, babe," he said, looking down at his phone.

When Albert finally made it to work, he walked through the lobby, got on the elevator, and stopped by Steph's desk.

"Hi, Steph, how was your weekend?"

"Hey, Albert! It was nice, my boyfriend and I went to the Museum of Illusions. It was really fun," she said excitedly.

"That sounds fun. Hey, thank you for the recommendation of the axe throwing place. I made a reservation for this week. It's Stacy and I's anniversary on Wednesday," he said

"Aw, that's sweet of you. I hope you two have fun! They have great drinks there too."

"Awesome. I'll let you know how it goes."

Must be nice... I remember when Stacy and I used to go out all the time.

Albert smiled, thinking to himself as he walked away. He opened the door to his office and dropped his bag on one of the chairs facing his desk. He sat down, turned on the screen, and started to look up the antique store they had visited over the weekend. He found their number on their website and decided to call to make sure the pendant was still there.

"Antique Showcase, how can I help you?" the old man said, almost screaming into the phone.

"Hi, good morning. I was in the store the other day and I saw a gold necklace with a moon pendant. Do you still have it in the store?"

"Give me a minute to check," the man said.

He put the phone down on the table and slowly walked around the shop looking at each table for the necklace. Albert sat on the other end, tapping his foot nervously as he waited. It took the man a few more seconds until he noticed it sitting in a box with other jewelry. He picked it up and walked back to the phone.

"Hello, yeah, we have it. It's an 1870s Victorian brooch in the shape of a crescent that was turned into a necklace. It's said to be owned by Caroline LeCount—"

"How much does it cost?" Albert asked, disregarding the history lesson the man was giving him.

"It's $350. Want me to hold it for you?"

Albert paused for a minute to think about how much money was in his savings account.

"Would you, please? I can be there later today to pick it up," Albert said.

"Sure thing. What's your name, sport?" the man yelled.

"Albert."

"Alex?" he repeated louder.

"No, Albert!" he screamed, trying to match his volume.

"Okay, Al, I'll hold it for you. Just to let you know we close at 5 today."

"No problem. I'll see you later."

Albert hung up the phone and shook his head as he thought about the conversation he just had. He sat there for a few moments before pulling his chair in and checking his emails. Even though he didn't have clients coming in, he had a budget proposal he had to finish and he needed to schedule a meeting with the executive team to discuss the firm's portfolio.

He had spent a few hours working on the proposal when he received an email from his boss, Gil. It was the announcement for the annual golf tournament. Albert sighed, knowing that he'd have to work hard this year not to embarrass himself on the course. He picked up his phone to check his schedule but was distracted by all the notifications. He scrolled through them, swiping each one away before opening up social media and mindlessly scrolling for a few minutes. Eventually, Albert opened his calendar to check the date. Moments later, a loud growl came from his stomach and he remembered that he hadn't eaten breakfast. Feeling a little sluggish and wanting a jolt, he decided to take a break and grab some coffee and a sandwich from the café.

Albert stepped into the elevator thinking about what limited options they had and wished he would start bringing his lunch more. He thought about the times when he and Stacy started to date and she would make him lunch and sometimes leave love notes. He stepped off the elevator and walked through the quiet hallway, smiling at Walter who was perched in his usual chair. The café had only a few customers and the music was the only sound besides the workers who were running around. He walked to the counter to look at the menu. He ordered a turkey and cheese panini, plain chips, and an Americano, and proceeded to slide down to the end after completing his order. A few minutes later, the cashier appeared with his food, he took his tray and sat down at the first table he saw.

He pulled out his phone again and started to text Stacy.

Hey babe, don't make plans for Wednesday night, I have something special for us.

He had just finished the text and was about to press send when he heard a familiar voice saying good afternoon to Walter. He turned around to see Becca walking up to him. He immediately put his phone down, turning it over to cover the screen, and waved hello.

"Hey! How's it going?" she asked.

Albert smiled, his face beaming with joy like a giddy child on Christmas morning.

"Hey! I'm good, grabbing a bite to eat. How was your weekend?" he replied.

She walked over to the table and sat down across from Albert. She put her large travel mug down and pulled toward her a chair to place her tan tote bag and computer next to her.

"Not bad. I have an assignment due today , so I had to do

---

a little writing.”

“What do you do for work?”

“I’m an entertainment and lifestyle writer. I write for Dai-lyDose Magazine. We cover celebrity news, food, and arts and culture.”

“That’s cool. What got you into it?” he asked, fully in-trigued.

“My mom used to take me to the salon a lot and I had to wait while she got her hair done, so I would read People magazine, and fell in love with the celebrity life. It was so amazing to me the way these people lived and I wanted to be a part of it, even if only from afar. When I got older, I started to write a blog about my favorite celebrities and their relationships, and that eventually led to this... What do you do on the fourth floor?”

“Huh,” he chuckled. “Nothing as cool as that. I work for an investment firm, Merrill Lynch.”

“Yup, I’ve heard of them. What made you want to go into finance?”

“The money...” he said, trying to be funny, but quickly noticed Becca didn’t laugh. “Honestly, I was always good at math and my dad constantly talked about the future and the importance of saving. I saved up for an entire summer to buy my first drum set.”

“Oh, that’s cool. Do you still play?”

“No, I wasn’t any good, but I loved trying to imitate my favorite artists. I like jazz music, so guys like Art Blakey or Buddy Rich were my idols.”

Becca nodded along with a smile, flustering Albert.

“Have you met anyone famous or had any cool experienc-es?” he asked, changing the subject.

“Last week I went to the premiere of *Hamilton* at the Kimmel Center."

"Whoa, lucky!"

"Yeah, and this Wednesday I have to review this hip new restaurant called Pearl and Mary Oyster Bar on 13th Street."

"Ooh, fancy," he said, sarcastically, hoping this time she would laugh.

Becca laughed a little, then looked at the clock on the wall and noticed that a half-hour had already passed.

"Listen, I have to run. I need to finish this before my five o'clock deadline."

"No worries, want to meet up tomorrow? Same time?" Albert said, the words jumping out of his mouth.

"Sure! See you tomorrow," Becca smiled, pushing in her chair as she grabbed her cup and bag and walked out of the café.

Albert sat there for a few minutes grinning to himself, thinking about what had just happened. He was ecstatic. He and Becca had just made a date to meet up the next day. A few days before that he had no idea who she was, but now they were meeting up to talk and have coffee together. He was so preoccupied by the conversation with Becca he forgot to eat lunch. He took a bite of his sandwich, realizing it was cold and the bread was hard, he decided to toss it out.

He hurried back to his office, hoping he didn't have any meetings that coincided with the time they were supposed to meet. He sat down at his laptop to add his lunch date with Becca to his calendar, typing in 'lunch meeting with a potential client' instead.

Looking over the rest of the week, Albert noticed the reminder in his calendar for his anniversary and remembered he was in the middle of texting Stacy. He opened his phone and clicked send on the message.

He sat back in his chair, sighed deeply, and put his phone

on his desk, ignoring the subtle guilt building in his gut. A few moments later, he heard a ding from his phone. He picked it up, thinking it was Stacy, but it was another email. He thought to himself if he should be concerned with Stacy starting to notice him dressing better and coming in early. He would have to think of a better reason than meetings with clients if he wanted to keep this up.

I'll tell her we're working with a new client on a huge proposal, that should work, he thought trying to ignore his growing worries, he turned his attention to the new email from Gil.

Great job on the proposal. I expect to see you on the course this year. Feel free to bring a friend!

Albert scratched at the base of his neck, knowing this was the second email from Gil about the tournament. He knew he couldn't avoid the tournament this year, but didn't want to continue the conversation so he simply replied,

Looking forward to it, sir!

P.S. Heading out a little early to buy a gift for my and Stacy's anniversary.

Albert sent the email and looked at the time, thinking he could catch an earlier train if he left right away. He answered a few more emails and closed out his computer. He grabbed his bag, walked out of his office, and waved goodbye to Steph.

Out on the street, he tried hailing a cab since the store was a five-minute drive away. It took him a few minutes, but a yellow cab finally noticed his tall frame with his hand raised in the air. The cab made a turn and pulled up on the corner right in front of him.

"Where are you going, bud?" the cabby said as he rolled down the window, wearing a baker boy cap and a flannel shirt.

"Corner of 16th and Pine, please," Albert said as he hopped in the car.

Ten minutes later, he was dropped off on the corner and walked to the front door of the small store. The bell on the back of the door rang as he opened it.

"Be there in a minute," the old man screamed.

"Take your time," Albert replied, looking around at the tables again, noticing all the new things he'd missed the first time.

He walked to the counter and the old man popped up from underneath the counter.

"Whoa!" he yelled, seeing Albert standing there staring at him. "How can I help you, son?"

"I called earlier about the necklace with a moon pendant. I believe you said you'd put it aside for me."

"Yeah, what'd you say your name was again, Al... Alex?"

"No, Albert," he said, shaking his head at the same time.

"Here it is," the man responded, oblivious to Albert's frustration. "Beautiful, isn't it?"

Albert nodded as the man put the necklace down on the counter and turned away for a second. He stood there staring at it, the gold, thin chain, and the brooch-turned-pendant and started to second guess his choice.

"Just a second, trying to find the right box to fit that," the man shouted out.

"What's the occasion?" he asked, picking up the necklace and slowly placing it in the small black box.

"It's my anniversary."

Albert reached into his back pocket to take his debit card out of his wallet.

"How many years have you been married?"

"Oh, we're not married, just dating."

The man punched in the number to the credit card machine and hit a couple of buttons on the old metal register. The

---

drawer opened and then the old man turned around and slammed it closed in a singular motion.

"Well, how long have you been dating this lovely lady?"

"It'll be seven years in a few days," Albert said, looking at his watch, wishing this interaction would end.

"What are you waiting for? You better marry that girl or she'll get away!"

"Yeah that's what everyone keeps telling me," he said sarcastically.

Albert grabbed the box before the man could say another word.

"Listen, thank you so much. I have to run, I don't want to miss my train," he said, already heading out the door.

Albert jumped on the train, sat back in his seat, and thought about the day. Thirty minutes later, he was blocks away from his house, and as he reached the door, he noticed the lights were still off. Stacy wasn't home yet, which meant he still had time to find the best hiding spot for his gift.

He walked in, dropped his jacket and bag next to the couch, and walked straight to the bedroom. He opened the closet door and looked for a spot on the top shelf. He saw an old pair of dress shoes he hadn't worn in a while and placed the jewelry box inside of it. He put the shoe box back on the top shelf and closed the door, but Albert did not hear the door open. Stacy was home and wondered why none of the lights as she walked to the bedroom.

"Hey!"

Stacy opened the door and when the knob hit the wall,

———————————

Albert jumped, hitting his head on the shelf in the closet.

"Who's there?" Albert called out, his voice a higher octave than normal.

"What are you doing in the dark?" she asked, flipping on the light.

"Nothing, I just got home."

"What's going on with you? You've been acting weird lately…"

"Nothing, I swear, still the same old Albert," he said, shrugging his shoulders.

"Okay, well I'm going to turn on the lights and get dinner started, sounds good to you?"

"Go right ahead," he said smiling.

CHAPTER 6

Albert was preoccupied most of the morning. He tried going through the motions of answering emails, but couldn't stop thinking about his official 'coffee date' with Becca. This wasn't another chance encounter; he didn't want to embarrass himself. He picked up his phone to look at the time before putting it down and turning it over. There was an hour to go.

This is taking too long, he thought, bouncing his leg up and down.

He leaned forward in his chair with his hand resting on his chin staring at the generic landscape painting directly in front of him.

He sat still, staring at the painting of a farmland with rolling hills and two trees overlooking a lake. The broken clouds littered the dismal blue-gray sky, meeting the hills in the middle of the painting. He followed the contours, his eyes moving up and down the undulation.

Albert had never thought much of the painting, but, at that moment, he found himself transformed by it.

I've never had a painting affect me this much... This must be how Stacy felt that day when we were at the museum, he thought.

Albert checked his phone again; it had been over half an

hour since he first started staring at the painting.

Oh, crap! I'm going to be late! he thought, leaping up out of his chair and grabbing his jacket before running out his office door.

Albert made a mad dash to the café, slowing down right as he was entering the lobby. He quickly looked at his reflection in the window, running his fingers through his hair trying to fix it a little. He walked in surveying the room, looking for Becca.

The café was busier than usual. Most of the tables were full of people talking, and the room smelled of arabica beans, making it difficult for him to focus. A few moments later, his eyes met hers as she sat in the middle of the room; she smiled as he awkwardly half-waved before walking up to the register to order. He grabbed his drink and walked over to the table.

"Hey! Hope I didn't keep you waiting," he said, pulling his chair out and sitting down.

"Hi, no worries, I just got here."

Albert smiled, unsure of what to say. He didn't want to seem nervous, but he felt himself wearing his nerves on his sleeve as his foot began to bounce under the table.

"How's it going? Did you finish *Rebecca* yet?"

"Yeah, it was really good. I love reading books a second and third time."

"Yeah, I feel the same way about movies."

Becca only nodded, causing an awkward pause for a moment before Albert decided to switch topics.

"Working on any fun assignments?" he asked, blowing on his coffee before taking a sip.

"Not right now, I should get a new one later today. I do have a side project I'm working on."

"Oh, really? What's the project?"

———————————

LOVE, TROUBLE & AMERICANO

57

"It's a column on the most promising restaurants of this year. I'm hoping to pitch it to my editor as a feature story."

"That sounds interesting... Good luck!" he said.

"Thank you."

Albert paused for a moment and looked around the café noticing that a few people had left as Becca picked up her travel mug and took a sip.

"So what do you do outside of work, Albert?"

"Not much really, I'm a homebody, but I do enjoy jazz music. I started collecting records when I was younger... You know, Coltrane, Mingus, Davis, guys like that."

"That's cool, you must have a lot if you've been collecting that long."

"I've always been into vinyl, but I never have time to listen to them."

"If you're ever in the market for new ones, there's a shop on South Street you should try. I heard they always get a new batch of records every couple of weeks," she suggested.

"I'll have to check it out," he said as he smiled, then took a sip of coffee.

"What do you do when you're not living the fabulous life?"

"I have a great group of friends, so, on weekends, we brunch or do something fun in the city, but, during the week, I don't have time when I'm on assignment. On weeknights, I binge-watch T.V. and read."

"Do you have a favorite show to watch?" Albert asked, wanting to learn more.

"Not really. I normally put on something I've seen before; I just like to have something playing in the background."

"I can understand that. That's one of the reasons why I

enjoy jazz; the music helps me concentrate."

"I feel that. So, you're a movie kind of guy… Have you watched any interesting movies lately?"

"Yes, the other night I stayed up on the couch watching this movie called *Delicatessen*. It's about a butcher who owns a run-down apartment building and is constantly in need of a repairman because the butcher murders them and feeds them to his customers. But his daughter falls in love with the newest repairman and is determined to save his life."

Becca looked at him with a bewildered face, as if she was unable to formulate a thought. Meanwhile, Albert's face lit up from describing the plot.

"I know it sounds crazy, but it's visually stunning and funny too."

"Okay, you've piqued my interest," she said as she picked up her phone to look up the movie.

She scrolled through the page on her phone before putting it back down.

"Good, now I've got something to watch this week."

"I think it's a pretty good movie, but that's just my opinion."

"No, thank you for the suggestion. I'll have to let you know what I think."

"Take down my number, and I can send a list of my all-time favorite movies."

"Okay," she said, picking up her phone again.

Albert recited his phone number as she typed it into her phone. He tried to hold back his excitement, elated to be able to talk to Becca more. She typed her name and a smiley face in a new message and sent it to him.

"There, I just sent you a text so you have my number."

The phone vibrated in his hand and the screen lit up.

"Got it," he said, the hairs on his arms standing up, his heart pounding.

Becca picked up her travel mug and shook it, checking to see how much coffee was left.

"I'm going to grab a refill, then head back up."

"Okay, no worries. I should get back to work too."

"This was nice," she said, getting up and pushing in her chair.

"Yeah, it's nice to have someone to chat with during my break."

As Becca walked over to get in line to order, Albert walked over to the counter and put his empty cup down.

"I have a meeting tomorrow, but I wouldn't mind chatting on Thursday or Friday if you have time," he said.

"Sure, let's do Friday. I may skip lunch tomorrow to work more on my story."

"Don't work too hard," he said, chuckling.

He hated how awkward he sounded.

"I'll shoot you a text on Friday when I'm coming down."

"Sounds like a plan."

"Alright, see you later then," he said, smiling and waving goodbye.

Albert walked out of the café toward the elevator, jumping for joy on the inside. He pulled his phone out of his pocket and looked at the message again. He went to save her in his contacts but then stopped for a second.

What if Stacy sees me texting her? She might get pissed and start asking questions, he thought.

He typed the name 'Bruce' in the name field instead of Becca and saved the contact.

Then, he opened up his notes app to start writing a list of his all-time favorite movies.

I'll just send her my top five... No top ten. I don't know... This is stupid, he thought.

He picked his five favorite movies in the order of when he first saw them and put the list in a message to Becca. He looked at it for a moment before hitting send and placing it back in his pocket. He pushed the button for the elevators and the loud ding rang over his head as the door opened.

CHAPTER 7

Albert awoke straddled by his alarm. He rolled over to turn the alarm off on his phone. Then, slowly got out of bed to get dressed. He opened the closet door and checked the spot where he hid the necklace for Stacy. Hearing footsteps, he grabbed a shirt and quickly closed the door behind him. He finished getting dressed and walked out to the living room where Stacy was seated with her legs crisscrossed, sipping a cup of coffee.

"Good morning, sweetie. Happy anniversary," she said.

"Morning, babe. Happy anniversary."

Albert walked into the kitchen to pour himself a cup of coffee and then walked back to the living room to sit on the couch next to Stacy.

"I'm working a half-day, and then I'll be home," Albert said, planting a kiss on Stacy's forehead.

"What's the plan for today?" she asked.

"I thought we'd try something new. I booked us a spot at this axe throwing place in the city."

"Okay, that sounds fun," she said excitedly, her eyes getting wider by the second. "Should I meet you at your office?"

Albert thought about it for a second.

What if Stacy and Becca run into each other? How would I explain that? Better not.

"How about I meet you at the store? I should be able to get there before one if you need to do anything before you close up," he said quickly.

"Whatever, doesn't matter to me," she said, shaking her head.

"We can exchange gifts tonight when we get home."

"Good, I still have time to get you something then," she said with a smirk.

"Funny, it better be a good one since it's last minute."

"Don't worry, I'll make sure to grab you something from the gas station on the way there."

Albert laughed, taking another sip of his coffee, putting it down, and then looking at his watch.

"What time is your train?"

"The next one is in twenty minutes... I'm going to finish this cup and get going."

"Okay, text me when you're on your way to the shop."

"Okay, babe."

Albert looked at Stacy sitting on the other side of the couch looking at her phone for a few seconds before getting up to put his cup in the sink. He walked back to the bedroom, grabbed the gift from the closet, and put it in his backpack. Then, he grabbed his jacket and walked back out to the living room.

"Alright, babe. I'll see you later."

"Okay, love you," she said, only slightly looking up from her phone.

"Love you too," he said as he closed the door behind him.

Albert spent most of the morning checking emails, push

ing off the assessment he needed to do for the company's new client. Around noon, he sent one to Gil telling him that he was taking the rest of the day off. He packed up his bag and headed out the door. When he walked past the front desk in the lobby, Steph looked up from her computer.

"Leaving early, Albert?" she asked.

"Yeah, I got a reservation for me and my girlfriend at the axe throwing place, " he said.

"I know, you told me on Monday… You okay?"

"Really? I'm sorry, Steph. I guess I've been a little preoccupied lately."

"It's okay, we all get wrapped up in our worlds sometimes," she chuckled.

More than you think, he thought.

"Well, have fun tonight, and try not to think about work," she replied, noticing Albert was lost in his thoughts.

"Thanks!" he smiled at Steph, then walked out of the office to the elevator.

When he made it to the lobby, he waved goodbye to Walter and walked out onto the street to catch a taxi. It was warm and sunny outside as he stood waiting. He took his phone out of his pocket to text Stacy that he would be there shortly. A few moments later, a taxi drove past and Albert quickly threw his hand up in the air.

"Corner of 13th and Sansom Street, please," he said to the driver as he got in.

"No problem. How's your day going?"

"Not bad, leaving early to take my girlfriend out for our anniversary."

The driver looked at Albert in the rearview mirror

"Oh, that's nice. What's the plan?"

"We're going axe-throwing."

"That's different, not your typical date night," said the driver.

"Nope."

"How long have you two been together?"

"Seven years."

The car stopped slowly at a red light and the driver turned around.

"Thinking about popping the question?"

"I don't know… I'm not in a rush, but everyone else seems to be," Albert said, slightly annoyed at the fact another person, a stranger, was pushing him about getting engaged.

The light turned green and the driver turned back around. Albert sat there silently for a few minutes; the driver noticed the awkward silence and wanted to break the tension.

"I'm sorry, I didn't mean anything by it. Sometimes I say stupid things."

Albert took a deep breath.

"It's okay. It's not your fault… You're just the third person to ask me this week."

"At the end of the day, it's your decision. You're the one who has to ask the question, right?"

"Exactly," Albert answered emphatically.

"Okay then. Don't worry, you'll know when the time is right."

"Thanks."

The driver stopped one last time, Albert paid the fare and hopped out of the taxi. He stood outside the shop for a moment, trying to shake off the conversation, not wanting to go in irritated. When he walked in, Stacy was standing behind the register helping a customer.

"Be with you in a minute," she said, not looking to see who came in.

There was only one customer in the store and there was light music playing in the background. The floor creaked as Albert walked around looking at the glass display case full of handcrafted jewelry. He circled past the handbags and other accessories on the shelves to look at the candles to the left of the register. He stopped to smell one while Stacy finished up. He popped the cap off and it smelled of eucalyptus and lavender. He put the cap back on, shaking his head.

"Hey, sweetie!" Stacy said, walking over to Albert who was standing in the middle of the store.

"Hey, how's your day been?" he asked, giving her a hug and a kiss.

"Not too busy, only a few customers... Just give me a few minutes to grab my stuff and lock up."

Stacy turned off the music and the computer, then reached under the counter to grab her purse. They walked over to the door, Stacy turned off the light, flipped the sign to close, and started to set the alarm.

"How far is it from here?"

"It's on 2nd and Market. We should get a cab."

They stood there for a few moments before he stepped into the street a little to hail a cab. They hopped in and Albert gave the driver the address. Fifteen minutes later, they were at the Kick Ass Axe Throwing and Bar.

The bar had a rustic feel, like a cabin in the woods, with elk heads hanging on flannel-lined walls. On one side of the bar were cages set up with targets, each stall equipped with a stump and a few axes.

Albert and Stacy walked up to the hostess stand.

"Hi, welcome to Kick Ass, do you have a reservation?"

"Yes, Albert H. for 2 at 2:00 pm."

The hostess grabbed two menus and walked from behind the stand toward the empty stalls.

"Your instructor will be over in a few minutes to go over everything. Can I get you a drink while you wait?"

"Yes, can I have a glass of white wine, please?"

"And for you, sir?"

"Whiskey neat, please"

"Sure thing, folks. I'll be right back."

The hostess walked away and Stacy and Albert sat down at the high-top table to wait for the drinks. The bar was full and each stall had a few people talking and throwing axes. Stacy looked around the bar enthralled by the place, surprised that Albert would pick such a unique date.

"What made you think of this place?" she asked.

"A girl at work told me about it."

"Oh, that was nice of her."

"She came here with her boyfriend last weekend and said they had a great time."

"This place is cool. Make sure you thank her for the recommendation."

"Yeah, I just wanted to do something different."

A young man in a polo shirt and jeans walked over to the table and introduced himself. He went through a few explanations and asked each one of them to step up to the stump and pick up an axe. He demonstrated how to properly throw and then asked each of them to take a practice throw. Stacy's first throw landed at the bottom of the bullseye.

'Whoa!" Stacy said as she threw up her hands.

"Not bad for your first throw! How about you try, sir?" the

<hr>

LOVE, TROUBLE & AMERICANO

instructor said.

Albert took the axe, raised it over his head, and held it there for a split second before bringing the axe forward and releasing it. The axe flung in the air and hit the top of the target.

"Huh," he said, surprised.

"That's okay, sir! Maybe next time try holding it a little longer before throwing it to give yourself more control."

"Yeah, thanks."

"Okay, guys, it seems like you have the hang of it. I'll be over here if you need anything. Have fun!"

"Thanks!" Stacy said, still thinking about her practice throw.

The hostess came over to drop off the drinks at the table. Stacy and Albert walked back over to sit down. They each sipped their drink and Stacy smiled at Albert.

"We should tell Rachel and Hunter about this place! Maybe next time we can do a double date here?"

"You think she would like it?"

"Why not?"

"I don't know, it doesn't seem like a place for her."

"She's more fun than you think. You should give her a chance."

"Okay, babe, maybe next time. Ready to go again?"

"Oh, yeah!" she said, hopping off her chair and over to the stall.

"I bet you I hit the bullseye."

"Lucky toss."

"We'll see."

She picked up another axe, stepped up to the line, and drew back the axe holding it in place then launching it forward and letting it go. It took her a second before she noticed.

"Bullseye."

"Nice job, babe," Albert said.

He was impressed at how quickly she picked up the technique and started to feel a little competitive. He picked up the axe, stepped up to the line, and tried mimicking Stacy's approach. The axe left his hands and hit the target right under the bullseye.

He walked over to the target to remove the axes and Stacy helped him carry them back to the stump. They went back and forth a few more times tossing the axes, Albert only getting slightly closer to the bullseye. Stacy hit dead center again, getting so excited that she screamed and jumped for joy with each hit. Albert, getting frustrated, walked over to the bar to order more drinks.

"I'll be right back, I'm going to run to the bathroom," Stacy said as he walked back to the table.

Albert sat down at the table, pulling out his phone to look at social media. A few moments later, he received a text from Becca:

Just finished watching Delicatessen, what a weird, yet beautiful movie.

He stared at his phone with his fingers hovering over the keyboard. His heart palpated as he typed the message.

What did I tell you? A classic love story.

He hesitated, reading it a few times before hitting the send button. Stacy had left the bathroom and was walking up to the table. Albert was so concentrated on the text, he'd forgotten he was on a date. Stacy saw Albert staring at his phone and put her hand on his shoulder to get his attention.

Albert jumped in his chair a little, lowering his hand. Stacy looked over his shoulder to see the name at the top of the messages.

"Who's Bruce?" she asked casually as she sat down and

<hr>

LOVE, TROUBLE & AMERICANO

took another sip of wine.

"Just a guy from work!"

He closed out the app and put his phone back in his pocket.

"Is everything all right?"

"Yes, he's new and was looking for a file on our new client."

"Do you need to go back in?"

"No, we're good. Today is about us."

He picked up his glass and finished his drink as Stacy threw another axe. They spent another half an hour throwing axes and laughing at how bad Albert was compared to Stacy. The instructor even joined in on the jokes, and normally Albert would have tried harder, but he was distracted by the text from Becca. They had one more drink and a few bar snacks before Albert paid the tab and they headed home.

Arriving at the house, there was a large box by the front steps, Stacy knelt down to pick it up as Albert opened the door. She dropped her purse and the box on the table and walked straight back to the bedroom.

"I'm going to get changed really quick."

"Okay, babe."

Albert walked into the kitchen, pulled his phone out of his pocket, and opened up the text message app. He undid the pending message to Becca and wrote:

Glad you liked the movie. Are we still on for Friday?

He closed the app and put his phone on silent before sliding it back into his pocket quickly. With a heavily beating heart, he walked back into the living room and picked up his bag to get Stacy's present. At the same time, she walked back into the living room in leggings and a tank top. She sat down on the couch, crossing her legs to face him. She placed the box on her lap, then held it out in front of her toward Albert with a smile.

"Happy Anniversary, baby."

"Happy Anniversary."

"I thought you forgot," he said.

"Nope, I ordered it two weeks ago," she said, proud of herself.

Albert smiled and ripped through the paper to reveal a Crosley record player. His eyes lit up as he read the side of the box.

"I know how much you've been enjoying your jazz music lately. I thought you might like a new record player."

"Thank you, sweetie."

"Do you like it?"

"Yes, it's perfect."

He turned to the coffee table and picked up the small black box and handed it to Stacy.

She held the box in her hand. Looking at the size, she didn't want to jump to conclusions. She took a deep breath and then lifted the lid off the top. The elegant gold Victorian necklace with a moon pendant lay in the box. Stacy saw it and recognized it immediately. She looked at Albert lovingly, so happy, he remembered a piece of jewelry she'd seen. She leaned forward, wrapped her arms around his neck, and kissed him.

"Can you help me put it on?"

She turned around and lifted her hair. He took the necklace out of the box and hung it around her neck then closed the clasp. The necklace fell on her chest and Stacy stared at it for a few seconds, feeling the pendant between her fingers.

She turned around again to kiss Albert. She looked him in the eyes, grabbed his hand, and led him to the bed. He stopped to

———

LOVE, TROUBLE & AMERICANO

to turn off the light before closing the door behind him.

PART THREE

CHAPTER 8

The lobby was bright from the sunlight reflecting off the glass windows, making large shadows on the floor in front of him. It was quiet other than the sound of cars passing outside. Albert stood motionless in front of the large garnet desk, staring at the text from Becca. He'd responded and was now contemplating if the exclamation point was too much.

Sure, same time in the café?

Works for me!

He heard footsteps and looked up as Walter, who had stopped watching videos on his phone, came from behind the desk to get Albert's attention.

"Are you okay, Bert? You've been standing like a statue for three minutes," he said, waving his hand in front of Albert's face.

"Yes… Yes, I'm fine. Sorry, I'm behind on a few emails and I'm waiting on a friend."

Walter nodded, then walked back around the desk and went back to watching the videos on his phone.

A few moments later, Albert saw the revolving door turn as Becca walked in.

"Hey," she said, still walking up, in a bright blue blazer, matching slacks, and black heels.

"Hi," he said, meeting her in the middle of the lobby.

The two walked into the café and ordered coffee; Becca also ordered a blueberry muffin. They sat down at their usual spot at the table in the center of the room. The square wooden table with modern metal chairs in pastel colors.

"Thank you again for the movie suggestion."

"Yeah, I'm glad you enjoyed it. I know it's not for everyone," Albert said, sipping his coffee.

"Would you like to share this muffin with me? I only like the tops."

"Sure. Did you know they sell only muffin tops?" he asked.

"Yes, I get them whenever I see them! I hate to waste, but the top tastes the best."

She took the top of the muffin and handed the bottom half to Albert, their hands touching momentarily. He thought he felt a spark like in the movies. Trying to contain his smile, he ripped off a piece of the muffin bottom and stuck it in his mouth, wiping his lips on the napkin before speaking.

"When I was a kid, I used to make muffins with my mom for breakfast. On Saturdays, we'd wake up and put on aprons, pull out all of the pots and pans, and make a huge mess," Albert said, trying to hide his blush.

"Awe, your mom sounds like a sweet woman," she said, taking a bite of the muffin top.

"Thanks."

The café was calm, with only one other patron seated in a booth reading the paper. The music overhead filled in the awkward silence.

"So, what do you like about jazz music?" Becca asked.

"I like the freedom the musician has. It feels like they're

free to do whatever they want, not like regular songs that have a set formula," he said with a light in his eyes, looking up and away as if a song was playing in his head at that moment.

"Have you ever thought about playing drums again?"

He'd forgotten he'd told her that detail about him. The fact she remembered made Albert feel heard.

"To be honest, I haven't thought about it until now. I miss it sometimes. I had to give my drums away when I went away to college. My parents couldn't hold on to them anymore. It would be cool if I had another set."

"Why don't you get another one?"

"Too much noise… I don't think my roommate would be happy."

"Girlfriend?"

"Nah, college friend," he said, immediately regretting it as soon as the words left his lips.

Can't take it back now, he thought, eating another piece of the muffin to stop the words from coming out.

"Well, maybe you should talk to them. Maybe they'll reconsider if you tell them how much you miss it."

"Yeah, maybe I will," he said, balling up the wrapper and placing it at the edge of the table.

"You look nice today," Albert said. "What's the occasion?"

"I have an event to cover, the opening of a show at the Walnut Street Theatre."

"Very exciting," he said, sarcastically.

"What?" she said, tilting her head inquisitively.

"Your life just sounds so much more glamorous than mine. It's stupid to say, but I'm jealous"

"Don't be! It's all fun and a good time until you have to sit down to write an article about it or create a recap video for social. Coming up with original ideas can be draining… Speaking of social, what's your @?"

Albert felt his heart stop beating for a moment.

Shit, I can't let her see all my pictures with Stacy.

"I don't believe in social media. It's just a bunch of people arguing and being rude in the comment sections."

"Sometimes, I wish I could be like people like you, disconnected. But I have to because of my job."

"Yeah, it's liberating not to be tied down."

"I can understand that," Becca said.

She picked up her phone and noticed the time.

"Shoot! I have to run, I need to prepare for a meeting in fifteen minutes."

"No worries, I'll clean this up," Albert said, looking up as Becca stood from the table to leave.

"Thanks, I'll see you."

"See you."

It is liberating not to be tied down. I mean, isn't it? No one to disappoint. No one to expect things from you, free as a bird to do as you please, he thought as he wiped the muffin crumbs off the table and took the coffee cups to the counter.

I bet things would be less stressful with Becca. I doubt we'd fight. Things just seem to come so easy with her. I bet it would be amazing. We'd probably have a stylish apartment in the city, we'd have impressive friends with interesting jobs, and we'd dine at all the fanciest restaurants in the city. On the weekends, we'll stay in and watch movies while we curl up on the couch eating moo shu pork…

Albert snapped out of his daydream, looking around to see if anyone noticed him imagining a life with someone who wasn't

Stacy. Seeing only Walter, his eyes glued to his phone, Albert looked back at the table, smiled, and walked out of the café.

———————

CHAPTER 9

Albert's phone vibrated on his desk. Text after text came in, but he refused to turn it over until he finished the report that was due in an hour. Sending the report to Gil, he closed the open tab and grabbed his phone. The texts were from Chad, Albert's grade school friend, about meeting up at Drinker's for happy hour. Checking the time, he clocked out early and decided to walk to the pub, sending Chad a message as he got into the elevator.

Sure, meet you there at 5.

Upon arrival, he looked through the large glass window and could see Chad was running late as usual. He'd only been in the bar once before and took a moment to look around before ordering a drink.

The walls were littered with antique beer signs. Albert sat at the long wooden bar with high chairs and saw the bottles neatly lined on the shelves. Two large TVs hung above the bottles with a large moose head in the middle. He chuckled to himself as the bartender walked over.

"What can I get you?"

"Whiskey and water, please."

The bartender returned with his drink. Albert took a sip and stared up at the TV still thinking about how weird and out of place the moose head looked on the wall. Halfway into his first drink, his friend Chad arrived.

"Sorry to keep you waiting, bro."

He waved to the bartender to get his attention. The bartender walked over recognizing Chad.

"Hey, man. What can I get you?"

"Can I get a beer?"

The bartender nodded and a few seconds later appeared with a cold beer.

"Thanks."

"So how's it been, man? Haven't seen you in a while," Chad said, turning toward Albert.

"You know, same old shit. What about you? How's your mom?"

"She's doing well, just went to visit her the other day."

"Tell her I say hi the next time you see her, and that I miss her chocolate chip cookies."

Chad laughed, spilling a drop of beer on his jeans.

"Man, those were the best, weren't they?"

"Too good! So, what's up with you and Ashley?"

"She's good, out with her friends from work."

"Cool, cool. How have things been with you two lately?"

"I don't know, man. It's been up and down for a few years, but I think we're on our way up again."

"Yeah, I hear you, " Albert said, nodding, taking a sip of his whiskey.

He sat for a minute staring at the bottles on the wall before asking his next question.

"What if you had someone pique your interest despite being in a relationship?"

Chad looked at Albert with a confused face, then turned back to his drink to take a sip.

LOVE, TROUBLE & AMERICANO

"I mean, as long as you're not married, play the field."

"What's going on with you and Stacy?" Chad added as he looked over from the TV curiously.

"We're good, the thought just popped into my head the other day."

"Hey, man, sometimes you gotta keep your options open."

The two men sat in the crowded bar not talking, just staring at the TVs, most of which were playing the Phillies game. The score was tied 2-2 in the bottom of the second inning. Albert ordered another drink—this time a double as well as a beer—and as he waited, his mind started to wonder.

Why did I ask him that? Doesn't matter, it's not like I'm cheating on her. Besides, it was a hypothetical question.

"Anyways... What else is going on?" Albert asked, taking a sip of his freshly poured whiskey, wiping ice off the beer bottle.

"Ugh, man, we just got invited to another wedding. That's the third one this year."

"What is with everyone getting married all of a sudden?"

"We're at that age now... All our friends are getting married, buying houses, and having kids."

"When are you and Ashley getting married?"

"Not any time soon. I'm kicking that can down the road as long as I can."

"Right?" Albert said, throwing up his hands.

"Be right back, I have to use the bathroom," Chad said as he stood up and started walking toward the back of the room.

Albert nodded and then stared up at the TV, not watching but thinking.

Why do we have to get married? Marriage is the beginning of the end. Once you put a label on it, then it goes rotten. We already live together and have been together for seven years.

What's the need to get married when everything is working perfectly? Besides, my parents spent their whole life together, never walking down the aisle and they were fine. My father always said, "Love is choosing to be with that person and dealing with them every day." I watched them have a long, loving relationship.

A few minutes later, Chad returned from the bathroom. The music in the bar was blurring and Albert was so deep in his thoughts that Chad had to repeat himself.

"Are you okay?"

"Yeah, yeah. I'm fine, just thinking. It's been a long week," Albert said, chugging the rest of his beer and finishing the whiskey in his glass.

"How long have your parents been married?" Albert asked suddenly.

Chad looked at him with confusion, but took another sip of his beer, brushing it off.

"I think they've been married for like 35 years, but they're old, man."

"How do you think they do it?"

"What?" Chad asked, turning to look at Albert.

"Stay together."

"I don't know, man. It's a pretty old fashion way of living if you ask me. Who says you have to be with the same person for that long?"

Albert went to take another sip of his beer, forgetting he had already chugged it.

I would feel trapped... It's almost like a prison sentence, he thought.

"Well, I guess at least they still love each other..." Chad said.

His comment had pulled Albert from his thoughts and left

---

him thinking about Stacy and how much he *did* love her.

He put his glass down at the edge of the bar, the bartender walked over, and Albert ordered another double and a beer too. His phone vibrated, and he reached into his pocket to take it out, it was a text from Becca.

Saw this video, thought you might like it.

She'd sent a video of Buddy Rich playing these drums, doing one of his famous solos. Albert's face flushed as he looked down at his phone watching the video he'd watched a million times before.

I can't believe she remembered his name, he thought.

He was so enamored with her and the fact that she cared and listened to him.

That guy is a genius. The things he does on drums are impossible!

"What are you looking at?" Chad asked.

"Watching a video of this guy playing the drums. He's amazing," Albert said, still watching the video.

Chad nodded and finished his drink. He stared up at the TV until Albert was done watching the video.

"Have you been to a game this year?"

"Not yet, we planned to go to one but didn't buy the tickets. They haven't been cheap since they've been playing well," Albert said.

"Yeah."

"I wonder if they'll go to the World Series this year," Chad said.

"We'll see. They're having a good run, let's not jinx it."

Albert looked up at the score and it was still 2-2, but the inning was now the bottom of the seventh. Almost two hours had passed since he'd been there and he'd not even noticed it.

"Hey, man. I'm going to have one more and then head out."

"Everything alright?"

"Yeah, Ashley just texted me and she needs my help with something."

"Okay, I'm going to hang out for a little bit."

"Cool."

They sat quietly watching TV as the happy hour crowd was starting to die down and the music changed to more upbeat pop songs. Chad guzzled down the rest of his beer and motioned for the check. The bartender walked over with the tab in his hand. Albert looked at his empty whiskey glass, and then ordered another double. Chad and the bartender looked at Albert.

"Are you going to be alright, man?" Chad asked, getting up from his chair.

"Yeah, I'm going to sit for a minute before I finish this last one. I'll be good."

"Okay, get home safe."

Albert sat there bobbing his head to the music, starting to think about Becca again.

Chad's right, just keep my options open. Who knows? Becca might like me. Besides Stacy and I have been together for a while, maybe things are getting stale and I need a fresh start.

Albert took a large gulp of his whiskey and looked around the bar. There were only a handful of people left. He looked at his phone to check the train times. The next train was leaving in 20 minutes. He had enough time to finish his drink and walk the five minutes down the block to the train. He took one last gulp and motioned to the bartender for the tab, before heading to the bathroom one last time. He paid his tab and walked out the front door. It was cloudy and cool outside, but the whiskey warmed Albert up as he

———————

LOVE, TROUBLE & AMERICANO

crossed the street and with every other step he wobbled a little.

He walked up to the plaza in front of City Hall and walked down the large steps. He made his way down the stairs and stood in front of the yellow line like always. Moments later, the train arrived and Albert stepped on, taking the first available seat. He put his head back and closed his eyes. Albert listened as the train sped down the track. He caught himself before falling asleep, his stop was next. He stood up, holding onto the bar until the train stopped.

He walked a few blocks to his house, humming the entire way. The song Becca had sent in the text message at the bar. He walked up to his door, fumbling his keys as he tried to open the door. He chuckled as he picked up the keys and hit his head against the door. It was so loud that Stacy got off the couch to see what the noise was. Albert found the key, but Stacy opened the door before he could put it in the lock.

"Albert?"

He stood there chuckling as he stepped inside.

"What's going on right now? Are you drunk?" Stacy asked, annoyed.

"Yes," he said, in a breathy voice.

"Ugh, you stink!"

Stacy was becoming more aggravated by the second.

"I can't stand it when you get like this."

Albert swayed as he walked through the living room to the kitchen. He opened the refrigerator door and grabbed a bottle of water. He took the cap off and took a sip.

"What? I went out with Chad and had a few drinks," he said, shouting from the kitchen.

"That's the other thing, I like your other friends, but not Chad."

"What's wrong with Chad? He didn't force me to drink!"

———————————

he yelled.

The two of them stood face to face in the living room next to the dining room table, Albert holding onto the chair for balance.

"But he sure didn't tell you to slow down," Stacy said, turning away from him.

"What's your point, Stacy?" he yelled.

"Can you please lower your voice?"

Albert bumped into the coffee table as he walked over to the couch, sat down dropping the water bottle down on the table.

"This is why. I hate when you get like this. Every time you go out with him, you come home completely wasted."

"Whatever, relax. It's no big deal."

"Don't patronize me. You're a sloppy drunk. Look at yourself, you can't even walk straight."

Albert rolled his eyes, struggling to keep her in his blurry line of sight.

"You shouldn't drink so much," Stacy said, standing in front of the coffee table and staring down at Albert.

"Leave me alone, Stacy, I didn't deserve this," Albert said, picking up the remote, turning on the TV, and increasing the volume.

"Fine, tune me out, Albert."

"What do you think I'm trying to do?"

"Whatever, I'm done fighting with you. Good night."

She turned and walked back to the bedroom with tears in her eyes. Albert stayed out in the living room as she crawled into bed, happy to have the living room to himself.

LOVE, TROUBLE & AMERICANO

CHAPTER 10

The sun seeped in through the blinds onto Albert's face. He woke up with his head pounding from a splitting headache. Stacy was already out of bed and he could faintly hear the TV playing in the living room. He rolled over onto his side, his stomach growled, and his entire body hurt. The result of having too much to drink and not enough to eat. He laid there, staring up at the ceiling, wondering when he had even crawled into bed.

Ugh, why did I have so much to drink?

He rubbed his eyes trying to get himself to wake up. He attempted to sit up, but became lightheaded and immediately laid back down.

Probably best to just stay here for a while.

Albert reached over to the nightstand to grab his phone and saw it was 7:50 AM when he remembered Becca texted him. He opened up the messages to see what his response was.

Good thing I didn't say anything embarrassing, he thought.

He placed his phone down and rolled back over, pulling the covers up over his face.

Albert woke up abruptly. Rubbing his eyes, he reached for his phone to look at the time. It was 2 PM. He checked his notifications. He had two emails from Gil and one from the office building management team. He opened the email and skimmed it, his eyes still adjusting to the light. He read the one from Gil telling him that Tyler was sick and asked why he wasn't in the office. Albert's head pounded harder at the mention of Tyler being sick. The annual golf tournament was next week. This was an important event and clients were going to be there, so he wanted to impress them. He needed someone to replace Tyler.

Albert sat up, his head still aching from his headache. He swiped to the next email. It was the building newsletter, reminding everyone that the costume party was a few days away. At the bottom was a note: **Be sure to bring a friend!**

Ugh, next week's going to be a rough one, he thought.

He got out of bed and stretched. It looked like Stacy has been relaxing on the couch all day. She seemed to ignore Albert as he walked out into the living room.

"Hey," he said, walking with his head down toward the kitchen.

"Hi," she said, without looking over.

"Listen, I'm sorry about last night. I didn't mean to get that drunk. I was at the bar and just lost track of time."

"Okay, Albert."

He took bottled water out of the refrigerator and walked over to the couch to sit down next to Stacy.

"I need a favor," he said.

"What?"

"Our company is having an annual golf tournament and I need to bring someone."

"Why?" she asked.

"My coworker Tyler is sick and won't be able to play. Gil is making me bring someone to impress our clients. I thought I could ask Hunter to join me. Last time we had dinner, we talked about golf."

"That's not a bad idea," she said, still avoiding Albert's eyes.

Stacy cleared her throat.

"What's the favor?"

"Can you give me his number?"

She lazily reached for her phone, clicked through her contacts, and looked for Hunter's number. A few seconds later, Albert's phone buzzed with Hunter's contact information.

"Thank you," he said as he opened the messaging app and started to text him.

"You're welcome."

Hey, Hunter, it's Albert, Stacy's boyfriend. I was wondering if you could help out, my company is having a golf tournament, and one of our guys got sick, want to join us?

He took the cap off his water and took a sip before asking his next question.

"Look, I know you're still mad, but there's a party in our building next week. It's a costume party, do you want to go?"

"I'll think about it."

He stood up from the couch, stretched again, and yawned.

"Okay, I'm going to hop in the shower. Then, do you want to go out for a little bit?"

"Sure, I could use a little walk."

Albert kissed her on the forehead and then walked to the bedroom. He undressed and got into the shower. His headache had strongly subsided and was feeling less hungover.

He stood there letting the water run dowh his back, thinking about the previous night, the text message from Becca, and his conversation with Chad. He wondered if he would see her at the costume party and if he should tell Stacy he couldn't bring guests anymore.

It's not cheating, I'm just keeping my options open, he thought as he worked the soap in his hair.

PART FOUR

CHAPTER 11

Albert stood in the bedroom, looking at his costume, about to get ready, while Stacy finished her makeup in the bathroom mirror.

She stepped out in a red sequined dress, red lipstick, and long purple gloves. She walked to the closet to get a pair of heels that matched her dress.

"Why did you pick *Who Framed Roger Rabbit?* I look ridiculous in this outfit."

"I like the movie, and don't act like you don't too. Besides you look good in red overalls."

"No one looks good in red overalls," he said as he adjusted his bowtie.

"Do I have to wear the bunny ears too?"

"Yes, it's part of the costume."

Albert put on his yellow gloves as he walked out to the living room. Stacy finished putting on her shoes and followed him.

"Are we ready?" she asked as she grabbed her purse.

"I think so."

The two grabbed their coats and Albert called a cab to take them to the train station. They stood on the platform and looked at the other people in business clothes, waiting for the train home from work. He felt ridiculous in his large red overalls. He could hear someone giggling a few feet from him. He leaned over to Stacy.

"I feel like the freaking Easter bunny."

"Halloween is around the corner, no one cares you're in costume."

"It's still like three weeks away," he said begrudgingly.

Minutes later, the train arrived and they boarded. They sat quietly as the train rocked back and forth on the track. The express train dropped them off and they walked the few blocks to his office. As they approached, he could hear the music playing. There were colored lights placed outside the doors to make it look like a nightclub. Albert could see a line and there was a man at the door checking a list. As he walked up, he noticed it was Walter dressed up in a well-formed suit.

"Hi, Bert!

"Hi, Walter, that's a very nice suit you have on."

"Thank you, it's the best I can do without being in costume. Have fun tonight," Walter said as he opened the door.

Albert and Stacy walked into the lobby. It was decorated with more lights and spider webs draped everywhere. The DJ took over the large granite desk and was bouncing to the music. The café was transformed into a bar and was offering spooky drinks. Albert saw Gil standing at one of the high-top tables and walked over to say hello.

"Hi, Sir, how is it going?" he said.

"Good."

"You remember my girlfriend, Stacy?"

"Nice to see you again," Gil said.

"Likewise," she said, shaking his hand.

"Do you mind if I talk to Albert for a moment?"

"Not at all," Stacy said.

Albert and Gil walked a few feet to the side near the wall to talk privately.

"Albert, you missed work the other day and didn't respond to any of your emails. Is everything okay?"

"Yes, sir, I'm sorry, I needed to take a personal day and I forgot to call out. I've been a little preoccupied lately," Albert said, lowering his head.

He hadn't noticed how focused he had been on Becca, how much it had begun to affect his work. He was ashamed this was the first time Gil had commented negatively about his performance.

"Well whatever it is, get it together. We have a potential client coming to meet us at the course at the end of the week. And speaking of the course, did you find someone to replace Tyler?"

"I have asked a friend of my mine, I'm still waiting to hear back."

"Don't disappoint me, Albert. You have a bright future here, don't suddenly blow it."

"Yes, sir. I won't"

"All right, enough of the serious stuff. How about you grab a drink for your lovely date?"

"That's a good idea."

They shook hands and Albert walked toward the café. Becca was walking out in a white dress, red lipstick, and a beauty mark. He looked at her and was stunned. His heart started to palpitate.

Oh shit, she's here, he thought.

He smiled uncomfortably as they stood in the doorway.

"Hey," she said.

"Hi, nice costume. Marilyn Monroe, right?"

"Yup, and who are you supposed to be?"

"Roger Rabbit"

"Ah, that's unique."

Albert laughed awkwardly. He was so disarmed seeing her standing there.

At that moment, Stacy looked across the room at Albert and saw how he looked at Becca when he talked to her. She stood there immobile as she looked at the woman.

"Can I get you a drink?" Albert asked.

"No, I'm good right now, but thank you," Becca responded, holding up the champagne flute already in her hand with a smile.

"Ah, right," Albert said, matching her smile.

"Grab a drink! We'll talk a little later!"

"For sure," he said, then awkwardly waved goodbye.

Albert stood in line, regretting having waved at Becca like a fool. When it was his turn, he order two glasses of white wine and walked back over to Stacy who was still standing in the same spot and had watched the whole interaction.

"Sorry about that, got caught in a conversation."

"I could see that," she said, pointedly.

"What?"

"Nothing… Thank you for my drink."

"You're welcome. There's a table open over there we can stand at," Albert said, pointing at the table with his head.

"What did you and Gil talk about?" she asked as they walked over and stood at the high-top table.

"He wanted to know why I wasn't at work and reminded me about the golf thing."

"Are you in trouble?" she asked, slightly concerned.

"No, it's fine. He worries when we have potential clients on the hook," he said, trying to sound reassuring.

———————————

The two stood quietly for a while, and Albert tried to ignore the subtle tension by surveying the room. Stacy pulled her phone out of her purse and started to scroll through social media. The DJ was playing "Monster Mash," there was a man dressed like Frankenstein dancing in the middle of the lobby, and the Bride of Frankenstein was making her way to the dance floor. Stacy laughed to herself as she looked at the two of them having fun together. Albert's concentration was broken when he heard clapping and cheering from across the room. He looked up past the couple dancing and saw Becca standing next to a man dressed in a Yankee baseball uniform. The two of them were arm in arm.

"I'm going to get another drink," he said, glaring over at the crowd.

"I'll come with you."

"Oh okay," he said, distracted as he walked over to the café.

Becca and the 'baseball player' walked over at the same time. The two couples met by the café and Albert started to sweat. His hands shook as he walked next to Stacy toward Becca. More people had joined the dance floor, and the lobby suddenly felt loud and claustrophobic.

"Hey, Albert! There's someone I want you to meet."

"Hey," he said, clearing his throat.

"Hi, I'm Becca."

"Nice to meet you. I'm Stacy, Albert's girlfriend."

Becca looked over at Albert, he looked down at his feet.

"Yes, I want to introduce you to my boyfriend—oh sorry my fiancé, Rick—it's still new to me, he just proposed," Becca said, raising her left hand with a smile.

"Hi, Rick," Stacy said.

"Hi, Rick," Albert added dejectedly.

———

LOVE, TROUBLE & AMERICANO

"Congratulations on your engagement, can I see the ring?" Stacy asked.

Becca held her hand out to show the diamond engagement ring.

Albert began disassociating. Stacy's reaction to the ring, Becca's comments, and the world around him went mute as he felt everything happening in slow motion. He felt beads of sweat beginning to form on his forehead. It was like his heart had cracked.

"Yeah, congrats," Albert said, snapping him out of the daze.

He couldn't stand there any longer, leaving Stacy to stand with the couple awkwardly.

"Will you excuse me for a minute," he said, wiping the sweat from his brow.

"You okay?" Stacy asked.

"Yeah, I'm fine. Just need to use the bathroom. Can you get me another drink?"

Stacy nodded, concern still present on her face while Albert beelined to the bathroom. He pushed the door open with both hands, then headed straight to the sink. He turned the water on and splashed some on his face to cool himself down. He turned the water off and took a few paper towels from the holder.

I can't believe she's engaged. Why wouldn't she tell me that... I mean, why should I be surprised? How much do I even know about her?

Albert dried his hands and tried throwing the paper towel in the trash but missed. He stood and looked at himself in the mirror for a moment. His floppy ears made him feel foolish. He thought about how he must have looked when he heard the news. One ear folded over and the other standing up.

I guess this means it's over between us. How could this

night get any worse?

He looked in the mirror one more time before he fixed his ears and walked, trying not to let the reality of his situation get to him.

Back in the lobby, Albert saw Stacy had gotten two new drinks and had brought them back to the table. Albert took a sip of the drink and turned to see Stacy who seemed annoyed.

"Should we go?" he asked.

"Yeah, I'm not having fun," she said, attempting to hide the irritation in her voice.

"Okay, let me say bye to Gil and we can go."

Albert found Gil and said goodbye, he reassured him that he would find a good replacement, although he wasn't sure himself. Then, met Stacy by the door and they walked out together.

"Leaving early?" Walter asked, looking up from his phone.

"Yeah, I'm not feeling well."

"Can I get you a cab?"

"Sure," Albert said.

Walter stepped off the curb and into the street slightly, raising his hand in the air. In seconds, a yellow cab pulled alongside another car parked on the street.

"There you go, you two have a good night," he said, smiling at Albert.

"Thanks, Walter, you too."

They reached the door to the house, Stacy opened it, turned on the light, and exploded.

"I knew something was going on with you!" she yelled as

she dropped her purse on the coffee table and took off her gloves.

"What?" Albert said, closing the door behind him.

They stood in the middle of the living room, Albert still with his head in a daze when Stacy turned around to face him.

"Don't play stupid with me, Albert. I saw you from across the room with Miss Marilyn Monroe."

"She's just a friend."

"Okay, that doesn't matter."

"What are you talking about?"

"You have a thing for her! I can tell," she popped back.

"You don't know what you're talking about! Besides, you just met her fiancé," he said, flustered.

"My intuition was right. I knew something was going on. The whole time I was worried that I was losing you, but I told myself, 'No,' and tried not to feel insecure and jealous."

He walked toward her and tried to console her, but she pushed him away.

"Tell me the truth, Albert. What's going on with you two? And don't lie!" she yelled.

"Nothing is going on," he replied.

"What did I say, Albert?"

"I'm not lying. We're just friends, we met in the café for coffee and talked. That's it."

"Are you serious?"

"What? What's wrong with coffee?"

"And I suppose you text each other?"

"Sometimes."

"You've got to be kidding me," she said turning away from Albert and walking into the kitchen.

She opened the cabinet, grabbed a wine glass, and started to pour herself a glass.

She was about to finish when Albert said, "I don't understand what the big deal is."

"How do you feel about her?"

"I don't feel anything about her."

Stacy took a deep breath before looking Albert in the eyes, hers demanding honesty.

He said nothing.

"I know you, Albert. You used to look at me like that. You're having an emotional relationship with her. You're cheating. Even if you didn't kiss her or have sex, you shared your heart with her. You *wanted* her."

"You're exaggerating," Albert said, putting his hands up in the air. "We just talked over coffee."

"I'm over it, Albert."

Stacy picked up her half-filled glass and took a sip, placing it back down on the counter abruptly.

"What's that supposed to mean?" he asked, confused.

"You don't know what you want."

"That's not true."

"I know you. You've been acting strange the last few weeks. Your mind has been elsewhere. You don't love me as much as I love you and I won't allow myself to be a settlement for you. You may not be able to have her, but I will not become your second choice."

Trying to hold back tears, Stacy walked to the hall closet and started to search for something.

"What are you looking for?"

"My suitcase!"

"Why?"

"I'm leaving. I… I need space."

"Are you serious?"

"Very."

"This is ridiculous! I can't believe you're making this into something."

"I'm not. You're just trying to pretend it's not a thing. Whatever. It doesn't matter. I can't be in the same house with you right now."

"Fine. Go, then."

Stacy stormed into the bedroom and flipped on the light. She threw the suitcase on the bed and started piling clothes into it while Albert furiously paced in the living room.

Let her leave. She doesn't know what she's talking about, he thought to himself.

He walked into the kitchen and picked up the wine glass that Stacy left on the counter. He pounded down the drink and poured himself another glass. Stacy closed her suitcase and stomped toward the door without saying another word to Albert. He stood in front of the sink and didn't stop her from leaving.

As Stacy slammed the door behind her, Albert finished the rest of the wine.

"Whatever. She's wrong. It's not cheating," he said to himself before he opened another bottle.

———————————

VINCENT J. HALL II

104

CHAPTER 12

Albert was in the lobby of the clubhouse checking his phone periodically, hoping Hunter would text him.

Where is he? he thought nervously.

As he was about to dial Hunter's number, his boss arrived. He opened the door, walked up the small set of steps, and into the lobby.

"Albert," he said, stopping at the top of the steps.

"Sir… how's it going?"

"Good… Where is your friend?" Gil asked.

"Stuck in traffic, but he's on his way."

Better to lie than to say I don't know, he thought.

"Okay, I'm going to stop in the bar and get a drink before we head out," he said, walking through the double doors into the bar.

Albert walked out of the clubhouse into the parking lot. He reached for his phone and was about to call Hunter when he saw a man he thought he recognized. Hunter walked up with his golf bag on his shoulder.

"Hey, man," Hunter said.

Albert felt a weight lift off his shoulders.

"Thanks for doing this," he said, shaking Hunter's hand.

"No problem," Hunter said, dropping his bag for a moment.

"Drop your bag off by the carts and we can go in and have a drink before we start," Albert said, pointing toward the line of carts parked on the sidewalk.

"Okay," Hunter said.

They walked into the clubhouse through the double doors to the bar where Albert immediately spotted Gil.

"Sir… this is my friend Hunter. Hunter, this is my boss, Gil Reynolds."

Hunter reached out and they shook hands.

"Nice to meet you."

"Same here," he said before following Albert to the end of the bar.

"Shall we get a drink?" Albert asked.

"Whiskey for me and a beer for my friend."

"Thanks," Hunter said

"First rounds on me."

"Okay."

They stood at the bar for a few minutes until the bartender came back with their drinks. Hunter took a sip of his beer and then looked over at Albert.

"So Stacy has been sleeping in our spare room the past couple of nights," Hunter said.

"Why am I not surprised? How is she doing?"

"It's hard to tell… She and Rachel sit in the living room, drink wine and talk a lot. Sometimes, they laugh, but I don't think they're talking about you when they do."

Albert chuckled to himself and then took a sip of his drink.

He looked at his phone to check the time, and at the same time, Gil announced,

"Okay, boys, drink up. It's almost time to start."

"Alright, let's head out and grab our cart," he said, pointing toward the door.

They walked back out the front door and down the path toward the line of carts where they found the cart with their bags tied to the back. Albert got into the driver's seat while Hunter sat down and waited for the other golfers to come out. A few moments later, everyone filed out of the bar onto the patio, Gil the last to exit.

Two speakers were set up on the patio for announcements, and the owner of the golf course handed him a microphone.

"Hello, everyone, thank you for coming out today for our annual golf event, a time for us to get out of the office and enjoy the sun. For those of you who don't know, this is a scramble. Starting with a tee-off on each hole, the team captain will decide on the best shot. Each golfer will then hit their ball from one chosen place and proceed likewise until everyone sinks their ball. Then, pick the lowest score for the hole and repeat. Look to your team captain if you have any questions. Good luck everyone, see you out there!"

Everyone applauded then got into their carts and drove off. Albert waited for the other carts to move and then started driving down the path. Hunter cleared his throat before speaking.

"Tell me your side of the story."

Albert sighed.

"It all just happened so fast... I met this girl who worked in my building. I don't know, something about her caught my eye and we just talked."

"Okay."

"It was innocent, you know? We would just meet in the café downstairs for coffee."

"Okay, so how did we get here?" he asked, taking a sip of

his beer.

The other cart pulled up with Gil and their potential client. Gil parked the cart, got out, and walked to the back to grab their clubs.

"Okay, gentleman, I'll start off," he said, coming around the side of the cart with his driver in his hand.

He put a tee into the ground, topping it with a golf ball. He stepped back and took a few practice swings before getting into position. He pulled back the club and swung, smacking the ball deep into the fairway.

"Not bad," Hunter said.

"Thanks, I play here often. Let's have our new friends hit after me."

Each one stepped up and teed off, the potential client, Hunter, and then Albert.

They all got back into their carts and drove down the pathway toward the hole. They stopped halfway, got out of their carts, and walked across the green to their balls. Albert looked and his ball was a few inches behind Gil's. Gil walked up behind him as he looked at the spot.

"Well done, Albert, keep it up."

"Thank you, sir."

The next few holes were the same, each of them teeing off, Gil out-hitting all of them. Hunter wanted to continue the conversation but didn't want to bring it up in front of the others. The group that was playing the next hole was taking too long, so they had to wait until they were done. Hunter felt like this was the best time to bring the conversation back up.

"So you had coffee with her. Was that it?"

"We texted a few times, but nothing really serious."

"Hmm."

———————————

"What?" Albert asked, getting annoyed.

"It sounds to me like you were starting to catch feelings for her," Hunter said.

Albert was taken aback. His face clinched up as he got frustrated.

"That's the same bullshit she said."

The group ahead of them finished teeing off. Gil and the potential client got out of their cart and started walking up to the tee box.

"I wasn't cheating. We were… just getting to know each other," Albert insisted.

"But did you want something to happen?"

Albert paused for a moment before answering, paralyzed by the question.

"Maybe," Albert said.

"So maybe you wanted a little more than friendship?"

Albert stayed quiet as he drove. He pulled up to the next tee box and stopped.

"Now imagine if Stacy did that," Hunter said, getting out of the cart.

He walked to the back of the cart and started looking in his bag.

That's bullshit. She would never. She loves me… But I would be mad if she was having coffee and texting some other guy, he thought to himself as he sat there.

"You might think you didn't do something wrong, but you have to stop and think how Stacy sees it," Hunter said, taking a club out of his bag.

"Come on, we're next."

Albert got out of the cart, went to his bag, and grabbed a club, preoccupied by Hunter's comment.

We barely hung out. It's not like I would have acted on anything, he thought.

He went up to the tee box, hit his ball, and sat back down in the cart. He hadn't even reacted to the fact the ball flew through the air, landing in a pond.

I know what cheating is, but… He's not wrong. I did want something to happen.

He played the next few holes the same way, completely in his head.

I wanted to see what life would be like with Becca and I hoped it would happen. What was I thinking? I messed everything up. Stacy thought we were destined for marriage, and I'm running away from her for someone who is engaged to another guy.

Hunter felt the shift in Albert's attitude. Even Gil started to notice him playing differently. Albert's last drive landed in a sand trap. Each time he swung, he would dig deeper into the sand until finally, after three swings, he was able to hit his ball out of the bunker.

Albert had one more hole to play through before they broke for lunch. When they made their way back to the clubhouse, Hunter went inside and Albert stopped to take his phone out of his bag to call Stacy. He called her phone, but it rang twice and went directly to voicemail.

He opened up his message and started to text her.

I'm coming over, we need to talk.

Albert felt a presence behind him. He turned around to see it was Gil.

"How's it going?"

"I've had better, I'm just not hitting well today."

"Evidently."

"Sorry, sir."

———————————

VINCENT J. HALL II

110

"It's all right. We all have bad days. Besides, your buddy seems to be doing well."

"Yeah, he's not bad. How's everything going with the potential client? Does he seem interested in signing on?" Albert said.

"Things look promising, now shake it off," he said, patting Albert's back, "Get some lunch and we'll regroup in a little bit."

Gil walked into the clubhouse as Hunter came back outside looking for him.

"Are you coming in for lunch?"

"In a minute," Albert said, checking his phone to see if Stacy had texted back.

He put his phone back in his bag and went into the clubhouse. They ate lunch and were back out on the course in under an hour. Albert tried to focus more on the game, but it was difficult. He was distracted by the thought he'd ruin his relationship with Stacy.

"You okay, Albert?" Hunter asked.

"I'm coming over when we're done, so Stacy and I can talk."

"What are you going to say?"

"I don't know, but I know I don't want to lose her. I have to think of a way to win her back. I can't lose her. I have to prove to her that I truly loved her and that Becca didn't mean anything."

"Sounds like you still need to prove it to yourself first," Hunter said before walking up to take his turn.

What has she been saying this whole time? That we should get married, and she's right. There's no one else like her, and I should have seen it.

He knew what he had to do. He played the last three holes more confidently, his attitude improved now that he had a plan. Gil

<hr>

LOVE, TROUBLE & AMERICANO

was happy to see that he was trying a little harder. He started to look like when they first started to play. On the last drive, his ball landed the furthest. When Gil added up their score, he chuckled to himself surprised.

"I don't know, we'll have to see who won when we get back. It's going to be close."

They all got back in their carts and drove down the path to the clubhouse, Albert following behind Gil.

"Have you tried calling her?" asked Hunter, breaking the silence.

"Yes, but it goes straight to voicemail, or it rings twice and then goes to the machine. I… I'm going to say bye to Gil and then head over. I don't want to get caught up in the awards. Do you mind holding on to my clubs?"

"I got you. I'll hang around for a little bit to hear the scores."

"What's your address?

"258 S. Bainbridge Street."

"Thanks, man. I appreciate you coming today."

"You're welcome. Good luck."

When they got to the clubhouse, Albert hopped out of the cart. He stopped on the patio to say goodbye to Gil who was waiting for everyone to come back to tally up the scores.

"Heading out already? We just got back, and haven't called the winner yet."

"Yes, sir. I'm sorry, but I have something important I need to do. I promise, after this things will be better."

"Okay, Albert. I hope so."

They shook hands and he walked through the clubhouse to the front parking lot.

Shit, I don't have a ring. Doesn't matter, all I need is an

---

answer. The ring can come later, he thought as he took out his phone to call a taxi.

A few minutes later, a car pulled up in front of the club-house. Albert got in hoping it wouldn't take long to get to the house. He thought about how he was going to start.

I have to apologize. There's no way she's going to take me back if I don't admit I was wrong. Then, I'll say I realized she was the one for me the entire time. That's it, I just have to make her see I made a mistake.

Ten minutes later, Albert pulled up to Hunter and Rachel's townhome with sweaty palms. He walked up to the red door and took out his phone to text Stacy he was there. He stood outside for a few moments, his heart palpitating with anticipation. When no answer came to his phone, he began knocking. Stacy opened the door moments later and stepped out slightly with the door still open behind her.

"What do you want?"

"I'm here to say I'm sorry."

She scoffed.

"I've been here for days and now you're showing up. I don't know who you are anymore."

"I know. I made a mistake. I don't know what I was think-ing. I was on the golf course today and I couldn't stop thinking about you and what I'd done. That I was ruining a perfect thing. You're the one that has always been there for me, and I'm sorry it took me so long to realize you've been the one for me the entire time."

Stacy didn't respond, just crossed her arms and shifted her weight to one side.

"I'm sorry I didn't see what I was doing was wrong."

"Clearly."

LOVE, TROUBLE & AMERICANO

"I get it now, and I would hate to think if you did that to me."

"Exactly, Albert. You hurt me."

"I'm sorry. I didn't mean to make you think I don't love you as much as you love me. Because I do. I love you so much."

"You going to have to do more than that to prove it to me."

"You're right, I've been missing the signs right in front of me. For the past seven years, you've been the one I've been with. The person who chooses to be with me every day and to love me, flaws and all. The one I share my memories with. The one I'm supposed to be with. It's always been you... I am willing to spend the rest of my life making that up to you."

"What are you talking about?" Stacy asked, stepping forward.

Albert took Stacy's hand, holding it tenderly. He bent down on one knee.

"I know I don't have a ring, but that can come later. We can go to the jewelry store and you can pick it out yourself."

"Albert, what are you doing?"

"Stacy, will you marry me?"

LOVE, TROUBLE & AMERICANO

ACKNOWLEDGMENTS

First and foremost, I would like to thank my readers, family, and friends. I greatly appreciate the love and support you show me every day.

To my wonderful partner, Meg, thank you for your continuous support and love, and for being my sounding board and listening to me talk endlessly about my story.

I would like to thank my publisher, Indie Earth Publishing, and my editor, Flor Ana Mireles, who worked tirelessly to make this perfect. Every project with you feels like a breeze. I appreciate the time and effort you put into making this a reality, and I look forward to our next project together.

Thank you to Yoanna Stefanova for taking the time to read this novella. I value your feedback, and your critiques were detailed and concise to help me make this better.

To Matt Nickles, Terry Lander, John Queor, Janelle Gianetta, Mise [ ], Dalila Fuentes, and Hayden Conley, thank you for reading. It's so delightful to see all the kind words you shared about my book.

ABOUT THE AUTHOR

ABOUT THE AUTHOR

VINCENT J. HALL II is a New Jersey-based writer who made his literary debut with *The Drinks Between Us*. A History graduate from William Paterson University, Vincent helps lead ArtPride New Jersey Foundation's advocacy and governmental affairs efforts. When he is not helping his community and advocating for arts and culture, Vincent enjoys attending Phillies games with his partner Megan, going to museums, and spending time with friends.

Connect with Vincent on Instagram:
@vincevangoah

ABOUT THE PUBLISHER

ABOUT THE PUBLISHER

INDIE EARTH PUBLISHING is an independent, author-first co-publishing company based in Miami, FL, dedicated to giving authors and writers the creative freedom they deserve when it comes to publishing their works. Indie Earth combines the freedom of self-publishing with the support and backing of traditional publishing for poetry, fiction, short story collections, and children's books by providing a plethora of services meant to aid them in the book publishing experience. A publisher for writers founded by a writer, with Indie Earth Publishing, you are more than just another author, you are part of the Indie Earth creative community, making a difference one book at a time.

FOR INQUIRIES, PLEASE VISIT
WWW.INDIEEARTHBOOKS.COM

INSTAGRAM: @INDIEEARTHBOOKS

www.ingramcontent.com/pod-product-compliance
Lightning Source LLC
Chambersburg PA
CBHW031147130726
47988CB00006B/2566